SURF
FISHING

SURF
FISHING

MARCUS SCHNECK

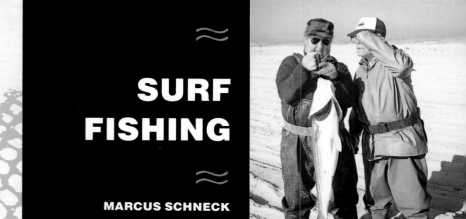

GALLERY BOOKS
An imprint of W.H. Smith Publishers Inc.
112 Madison Avenue
New York, New York 10016

A QUINTET BOOK
produced for
GALLERY BOOKS
An imprint of W.H. Smith Publishers Inc.
112 Madison Avenue
New York, New York 10016

ISBN 0-8317-6435-X

This book was designed and produced by
Quintet Publishing Limited
6 Blundell Street
London N7 9BH

CREATIVE DIRECTOR: Terry Jeavons
ART DIRECTOR: Ian Hunt
DESIGNER: Anna Brook
PROJECT EDITOR: Sally Harper
EDITOR: Rosemary Booton

ILLUSTRATOR: Danny McBride

Typeset in Great Britain by
Central Southern Typesetters, Eastbourne
Manufactured in Hong Kong by Regent Publishing Services Limited
Printed in Hong Kong by Leefung-Asco Printers Limited

CREDITS

Frank S. Balthis: pages 6, 10 t, 13, 22 t, 23, 29 t, 31 t, 32 t, 39 l,
40 t, 40 b, 43 t, 43 b, 44 br, 46, 55, 71, 86, 87.

Jill Barnes: pages 43 c, 88.

Myer S. Bornstein: page 38 t.

M. Fifield: pages 37 r, 58 b, 68.

Ed Jaworowski: pages 4, 14, 16 t, 16 b, 18 b, 20 t, 20 b, 21 b, 29 b, 36 b,

38 bl, 41 t, 42 b, 44 tr, 49 tl, 49 tr, 57 b, 58 l, 78, 79, 80.

Walt jennings: pages 52 t, 56 l, 57 t, 61 l, 64, 65 t, 85.

Joe Malat: pages 9 l, 10 b, 11 t, 11 b, 22 b, 24 t, 25, 27 t, 30 b, 31 bl, 53.

Dick Mermon: pages 2, 8, 9 r, 12, 18 t, 19, 24 b, 27 b, 30 t, 31 br, 32 bl.

32 br, 33 l, 37 l, 38 br, 39 r, 42 t, 48, 49 bl, 49 br, 50 t, 52 b, 56 r.

58 r, 59, 61 r, 62, 63, 65 b, 66, 73, 82, 83, 90, 91, 92.

Mike Millman: front cover.

Paul Pavlik: pages 17 b, 33 r, 36 t, 44 l, 60, 93 t, 93 b.

Scott Weidensaul: pages 17 t, 21 t, 21 c, 34, 41 b, 50 b.

CONTENTS

INTRODUCTION

You have to be a bit of a masochist to enjoy surf fishing. Nearly every element that Nature can muster is thrown against you, from a constantly changing landscape under the water, through harsh weather that confines all saner individuals to the warmth of their homes, to finicky, relocation-prone fish.

There are certainly easier ways to catch fish in the ocean. Party boats and charters return with huge coolers overflowing with catches in the hundreds; yet veteran surf fishermen struggle through the entire day for even a fair number of the same species of fish. A large fish caught in the surf must be fought toe-to-toe, so to speak, while that same fish could be pursued with a boat to give the angler a much easier time of hauling it in.

And yet, surf fishing enjoys a tremendous following across the United States and portions of Canada. Many of the same adversities and hardships already outlined are also some of the attractions of this primeval sport for many of its most ardent followers. The sport presents one of the greatest challenges in the sporting world, with even the most veteran among our ranks learning something new on nearly every outing. When that old-timer thinks he has just about every trick in his book and knows nearly every pebble on his favorite beach, Nature will toss a major storm into the mix, changing that beach completely.

A fish taken in the surf, almost without exception, will deliver a better fight than the same species, the

same size, taken from a boat. That fish in the surf also finds a far greater abundance of obstacles to snag, rip, and otherwise destroy the fishing line. In addition, variety both in species and size is virtually unmatched in any other watery environment on Earth.

Surf fishing is also one of the least discriminatory forms of fishing. After the initial investment in proper equipment there is very limited additional advantage that more money will buy. Boat ownership or chartering is not necessary. There are only so

ABOVE

Most surf fishing today is
done in far less remote and
wild locations than this fish
camp along the northern
Pacific coast of Canada.

RIGHT

The simple, unpainted
metal spoons and jigs have
proven themselves millions
of times, over many
generations.

many lures and baits that anyone can hurl into the
surf on any given day. Experience and skill remain
the only factors that consistently separate successful from less successful surf fishermen.

Man has been angling in the surf – in one way or
another – since our primitive ancestors first ate what
they found cast onto the beaches by the waves.
Spears and crude traps of many descriptions followed later in man's development, allowing for a
more efficient and less haphazard approach to har-
vesting the bounties of the ocean.

RIGHT

These bluefish were taken on a topwater plug (top) and a Hopkins lure, which runs deeper.

BELOW

Nearly anything cast into this passing school of bluefish will bring an almost immediate strike.

The earliest records – well before the advent of the written word – of the use of hook and line in the surf are found in Europe. A forked stick was used to hurl a weight and baited hook out into the water, with the line "reeling" off a curled pile at the angler's feet.

Native Americans were tapping the wealth that the oceans had to offer long before any European foot had touched North American soil, but the first written record of surf fishing in the "New World" belongs to the settlers in the New England area. Less than a decade after the Pilgrims stepped off the *Mayflower* at Plymouth Rock in 1620, striped bass were being caught from the surf. The records indicate that lobster was the preferred bait. Like every activity that filled the colonists' long days, surf fishing was done for the sole purpose of providing food. Any means that would bring the fish to the larder were employed. Sport was generally not a major consideration.

Surf fishing more on the order of the sport that we know today got its true start in the second half of the 19th century. Wealthy businessmen and industrialists turned their attention to the sport, traveling from the cities of the Northeast to favorite haunts along the coasts of Massachusetts and Rhode Island.

These anglers formed the first fishing clubs, exclusive affairs with high admittance fees and posh conditions. Platforms were erected some distance out into the water, with planked walkways leading comfortably to them.

Stripers were once again the target fish. Lobsters and menhaden (bunker) were the bait, placed on the hook by assistants, who also chummed the waters with discards. Bamboo rods of 7 to 9 feet and the largest available freshwater reels were rigged with heavy linen or silk line.

As the 20th century dawned, surf fishing was becoming a much more popular and less exclusive pursuit, as Americans were earning more leisure time and more discretionary cash, and the automobile was making personal transportation an everyday event. Tackle and lure manufacturers responded, mass-producing the equipment that this new buying public wanted. Stripers remained the most sought-after species.

Today an amazing array of species occupy the interests of the very diversified surf-fishing fraternity. Some anglers choose to specialize in a few species, while others content themselves with casting for whatever happens to be available and hitting at the moment.

Although the sport attracts fewer anglers than almost any other form of fishing on the North American continent, millions flock into the surf each year and the number is growing.

LEFT
A moment shared: there's
more to any sport than the
catch or the kill.

≈

TACKLE

LEFT
The sign of a serious surf
fisherman a vehicle rigged
for action.

≈

When it comes to tackle and gear for surf fishing, like most forms of fishing, the angler can choose to go as elaborate and expensive, or as simple and cheap, as he wants. Thousands of dollars can be plunked onto the tackle dealer's counter for more equipment than the average angler would use in a lifetime, or a few hundred can be spent for just the right gear to get started. Neither approach is wrong. Neither is guaranteed to catch fish.

Some once- or twice-a-year surf fishermen even make do with heavy freshwater gear that they have on hand for other fishing action. While this may be the cheapest approach to trying the sport, it is practically a sure thing that these anglers will not get into all that many fish and they probably won't enjoy the sport enough to try it again. The surf environment, complete with a constant salinity in the air, will be hard on freshwater equipment that is not designed for use here. While the line between equipment for the two sports has been blurring in recent years with the introduction of new materials, only the very best freshwater gear can be expected to

function for very long, under marine conditions. And, why would someone with the most expensive, high quality freshwater equipment want to dunk it in the ocean?

The angler who wants to try a few outings before committing to the purchase of yet another type of gear might want to rent proper surf equipment a

ABOVE
Flyfishing becomes more
popular each year in the
surf as an exciting,
exacting way to take fish.

≈

Jetties provide access to
much deeper water than
the surf angler could
otherwise reach.

Today's surf-fishing
equipment is better
designed to withstand the
harsh rigors of the marine
environment.

ation that is best suited to one form of surf fishing can vary considerably from that needed for another form of the sport.

For example, the angler planning to do a great deal of his fishing from jetties, reefs, points, cliffs and the like can get away with a shorter rod. By using the various structures described here to get further out into the ocean, he will lessen the casting distance needed to reach desired spots and thus the length of rod needed. On the other hand, the angler who will be casting most often from sandy beaches will need the added casting power and distance that a longer, heavier rod affords. This bigger rod also lends more power in battling large fish or fishing against heavy water.

While some purists continue to struggle with the old-style, birdnest-prone surf-casting reels, most anglers today have turned to spinning reels that are much easier to use and that are produced in a variety of surf-fishing models. These reels are designed with strong parts made of non-corrosive materials that can stand up to the rigors of the sport.

couple of times. Rented gear is not generally the best you can find, but it will do the job while the angler gets a taste of surf fishing.

When a decision is eventually made to move fully into this strange form of fishing, the very next consideration must be the location that the angler plans to fish most often. The rod, reel and line combin-

the largest of surf spinning reels able to hold as much as 400 yards of 20- to 25-pound-test monofilament line. Bait rigs and lures of as much as 5 ounces can be tossed about with this combination.

You will notice that in all references I have pointed to monofilament line. This is the standard in today's sport, and manufacturers are making it better every year. Today's line is thinner and stronger giving the kind of casting distance that our fathers could not hope to achieve.

LEADERS

But surf fishing requirements do not stop with the line. Surf is an extremely unforgiving environment to be fishing in, and the chances of nicks, scrapes and the like on a line are quite high. To lessen these impacts to the monofilament, surf fishermen generally use a "shocker" leader. As the name implies, this extra length of line absorbs the shocks of surf

ROD-REEL
COMBINATIONS

ABOVE

Many surf fishermen prefer very long, stiff rods to allow for maximum casting ability.

RIGHT

Many anglers today have chosen to move to lighter tackle for some species, such as striped bass.

For surf fishing these combinations fall loosely into three categories:

LIGHT COMBINATIONS consist of a relatively light-action rod of 8 to 9 feet in length, one of the smaller surf-spinning reels and 250 yards of 10- or 12-pound-test monofilament line. This rig will handle lures and baits weighing as much as 2 ounces or slightly more.

MEDIUM COMBINATIONS move up to a stiffer-action rod of 9 to 10 feet in length and a medium-to-large surf-spinning reel with 300 to 350 yards of 15- to 20-pound-test monofilament line. Bait rigs and lures up to about 3 ounces will work nicely on this combination.

HEAVY COMBINATIONS are necessary for the largest surf fish, such as big striped bass or sharks. These team a 10- to 14-foot rod of stiff action with

decide to stay with monofilament in still heavier pound-test to gain as much in-water line invisibility as possible.

POKE-POLING

This technique is rumored to have developed along the Californian coast, on the shoreline of Sonoma and Marin Counties. Poke-poling is done with 12- to 15-foot bamboo poles that allow the angler to place the bait between wash rocks and into deep tide pools, especially where the surf is likely to surge over the rocks. At the end of the pole, a 3- to 4-foot piece of wire is attached to a 4- to 6-inch piece of heavy leader of chalk line, terminating with a 2/0 or 4/0 hook that is baited with abalone, mussel clam, shrimp or cut fish.

LURES

Artificial lures are available in an incredible array of designs, colors and materials today. Few anglers could afford to carry everything that's available in even a small tackle shop; however, there are a few families of lures that should be represented in every surf angler's tackle bag or box.

METAL SQUIDS are intended as imitations of various baitfish. They are available in many shapes other than the namesake squid and in weights ranging from ½ to 5 ounces. They come equipped with stationary hooks or swinging hooks. Some anglers add a brightly colored strip of pork rind to the swinging-hook types to give them added fish-attracting power.

fishing. Heavier monofilament, as much as 50-pound-test, is used for this purpose in lengths of 12 to 15 feet. This "shocker" leader is attached to the front of the regular monofilament line, with the bait rig, lure and so forth attached to the opposite end of the leader.

Opinion is divided on the correct material to use for the "shocker" leader against the toothier fish such as shark, barracuda, bluefish and mackerel. Some anglers prefer wire leader, a single-strand stainless steel of No. 8 to No. 10. Other fishermen

ABOVE
Reels that can handle lots of line are desirable for surf fishing, where casting distance can be crucial.

≈

ABOVE

The flyrod popper with fly trailer (top) is effective for weakfish. The fish fry, cut bait and shrimp flies (middle left to right) are generally cast into chum slicks for best results.

BELOW

A wide variety of "swimming lures" have been developed for the highly popular striped bass, including this selection of designs and color patterns.

SURFACE PLUGS are designed to create a commotion on the surface of the water. Examples include poppers and thin minnows. Their action mimics that of injured or pursued baitfish, which often break the surface in attempts to escape.

DIVING/FLOATING PLUGS are intended to do the same kind of imitations as surface plugs, but under the water. They are available in an incredible range of colors, patterns and body shapes, as well as abilities to dive to different depths.

LEAD-HEAD JIGS incorporate feathers, fur or strips of plastic into their tails to create their imitations of baitfish. They can be painted in a wide variety of colors and patterns, and come in weights varying from about ½ ounce to more than 3 ounces.

PLASTIC EELS have been developed to imitate just about everything a fish could want to eat in saltwater, as plastic worms do in freshwater. They are produced in many color variations and in lengths ranging from 8 to 15 inches. (A short-tailed version is also offered for use behind a lead-head jig.)

In the use of any artificial lure, an important first consideration should be the type of baitfish swimming in the waters to be fished. The angler doesn't have to make an exact species identification of the

JIGS FOR CASTING AND DEEP FISHING

A. The dart jig planes actively when being retrieved.

B. A 'Japanese' rig is shown here undressed, to expose the leader wire which slides through the head and is attached flexibly to the hook. This design allows the head and dressing to move up on the wire when a fish is taken.

C. The flat sides of the Lima Bean jig allow it to swing with the movement of the water.

D. The keeling jig has a flattened base and is good for bottom feeders.

E. The bullet jig is a good all-rounder.

small fish he observes swimming in the surf, but a close match between artificial and living patterns should enhance the fish-attracting power of the artificial.

Some anglers add a strip of pork rind or a small baitfish to their lures for added appeal and to give the fish a "taste" of something real and natural when it strikes. In bait fishing, we are already using the living baitfish so this need not be a concern.

TACKLE

21

LEFT

Many spoon designs have been created to mimic baitfish species commonly found in the surf. Other designs aim to catch attention through their unnaturally bright colors.

HOOKS

The most basic element of any type of bait fishing is the hook. For surf fishing, this usually means hooks varying in size from the No. 4 to the 8/0 depending on the size of the fish being sought. Many manufacturers today produce an almost limitless array of variations on the hook design, each variation touted to offer some special advantage. Personal preference and experience must be each angler's guide, with one qualifier: any hook to be used in a saltwater environment should have some sort of anti-rust finish, such as cadmium plating, gold plating or stainless steel.

CENTER RIGHT

This needlefish imitation appears much like the living baitfish it was designed to imitate, while the chartreuse Bomber relies more on its bright color.

RIGHT

By comparison to the horseshoe bite-mark of a bluefish on this baitfish, the 5-inch streamer fly seems small.

SINKERS

Otherwise known as weights, these come in fewer variations than hooks, but the different designs may perform more of a real function than many of the hook-design alterations.

BANK is torpedo-shaped with the eyelet at the tail end. This is a good weight to use in rocky areas because it tends to bounce off obstructions rather than snagging onto them.

ROUND is shaped exactly as the name implies. This can be even less prone to snags in rocky areas, bouncing off and around objects quite naturally.

PYRAMID is designed for use in sandy beach areas. It provides a solid anchor for bait fishing, but

LEFT

A sand spike can relieve
and free the angler's arms
for those long waits
between strikes.

should be avoided in rocky areas because it snags on just about any obstruction.

BULLDOZER is shaped like a T-bone steak. With the eyelet inside the curve of the T-bone, the bulldozer weight digs into the sand, providing a rock-solid anchor in a sandy beach area, but a sure and certain snag in any area with obstructions.

EGG is egg-shaped with a hole running lengthwise through its center. This weight is generally slipped over the monofilament line before the hook or other terminal tackle is attached. It is held away from the hook area with a split shot on the line. The egg sinker is used to provide weight to get down to the bottom while allowing a fish to pick up the bait and run with it without immediately feeling the drag of the weight. As the fish runs with the bait, the line pulls through the egg sinker, which remains firmly in place.

SAND SPIKES AND ROD BELTS

There are a few pieces of equipment that will make bait fishing in the surf more enjoyable, although they are by no means essential for someone who is just starting out.

The sand spike is a hollow tube equipped with a pointed shaft at one end. The shaft is thrust down into the sand to provide a stable base for the tube to hold the butt of the fishing rod. This frees the angler from holding the rod for extended periods while waiting for a bite. It is also used by fishermen fishing with artificial lures, to hold their rods upright while they change lures or make other adjustments to the terminal end of the line.

A rod belt does much the same thing as a sand spike, but is attached around the waist of the angler. It also can be used to reduce the strain of casting and lessen the impact on the arms in fighting a fish. That may not sound all that important to the novice, but the veteran who has spent days endlessly casting into the surf will have a different opinion.

RIGS

≈

A few simple bait fishing rigs do most of the work for surf fishermen.

STANDARD SURF RIG This attaches a three-way swivel to the end of the monofilament line, a sinker on a short leader to the second of the three eyelets and the hook on a 3-foot leader to the third.

LEFT
A flounder with the bait-rig
on which it was taken: the
two-hook bottom rig.

TWO-HOOK RIG This is preferred by many surf anglers to the standard surf rig because of the additional possibilities offered by presenting more than one bait at a time. A pyramid sinker is tied to the end of the monofilament line. Immediately above the sinker, a hook at the end of a 2-foot leader is attached to the line. About 2 feet further up the line a second hook on a shorter leader (1 to 1½ feet long) is attached to the monofilament line.

When using this rig into a school of fish that has been seen and identified, the same bait – a type that is known to produce on this species of fish – can be placed on both hooks, in an attempt to take two fish at one time. When the rig is being used to locate fish and to discover what they're attracted to, a better bet is to use different baits on each hook, to give them a choice.

FISH-FINDER RIG This is a commercially produced device with an eyelet at one end of a short length of metal and a snap at the other. The monofilament line is run through the eyelet and tied to the "shocker" leader via a simple two-ended swivel.

Hook and bait are attached at the opposite end of the "shocker" leader. The sinker is attached to the snap on the fish-finder rig.

When the fish takes the bait and runs with it, it will not feel the weight of the sinker as the line slips through the fish-finder eyelet. This aspect means that the fish-finder rig offers advantages similar to those provided by the egg sinker.

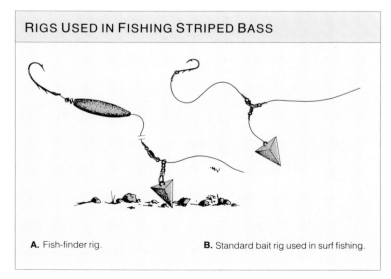

RIGS USED IN FISHING STRIPED BASS

A. Fish-finder rig.   **B.** Standard bait rig used in surf fishing.

CASTING TECHNIQUES USING CONVENTIONAL TACKLE

A. Stand with your left shoulder toward the water, at right angles to the line of cast (left-handed anglers should reverse these directions).

B. Rotate your body to the right while lowering the rod and extending it directly away from the direction in which you will cast. Your weight should be on the right foot.

C. As you begin to cast, shift your weight to the left foot. Watch the lure while applying force with your arms.

D. Continue to shift weight forward; the force in your arms will make the rod bend deeply. Rotate your head in the direction of the cast.

E. At the peak of the movement, the right arm pushes forward with the rod as the left hand pulls back on the butt.

F. Follow through in the direction of the cast; this keeps friction between the guides and the line to a minimum.

BAITS

In the following discussion of natural baits, the angler should take into consideration any restrictions on bait gathering and any limits imposed by fisheries agencies with jurisdiction over the area he intends to gather or use those baits.

EELS For many years, eels were the top natural baitfish among surf fishermen, particularly those in search of big striped bass. Although the slippery creatures remain high on the list of best baitfish, they have become increasingly difficult to find naturally or to purchase at bait shops. When they can be had, they are hooked with one or two hooks that then protrude from their underside. They are usually fished on or near the bottom – their natural habitat – with weights to hold them down. Some

LEFT
Pieces and fillets of nearly any fish species are effective baits for many species of gamefish, such as this bluefish that fell to a mullet head.

BELOW
Sand eels are generally easy to locate on any sandy beach and they make deadly bait for both small surf gamefish, when fished individually, and larger species, when several are placed on the same hook.

METHODS OF HOOKING BAIT

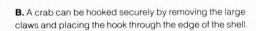

A. Shrimp may be hooked behind the eye through the shell (top) or through the tail; the barb may face up or down.

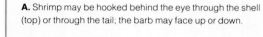

B. A crab can be hooked securely by removing the large claws and placing the hook through the edge of the shell.

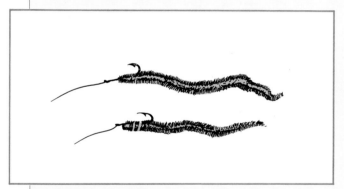

C. There are two ways of hooking a seaworm: (top) place the barb in the mouth and bring it through about an inch behind the head; or (below) tie the worm to the hook with small rubber bands in order to keep the worm alive.

D. Live baitfish may be hooked in three ways: (from top) behind the head above the backbone; through upper lip or both lips; or with a double hook arrangement.

RIGHT
Finger mullet are one of the
most popular baitfish along
the Atlantic coast for
striped bass and bluefish.

ABOVE
Throw-netters are a
popular and effective
means of catching baitfish
in the surf.

surf anglers also find success by fishing eels a few feet behind a float.

In a marriage of artificial and natural baits, some anglers stretch eel skins over metal squids or other similar lures.

MULLET The common name of mullet is applied to one of the most common baitfish available to surf fishermen today. Of this large family of fish, only the striped mullet and white mullet are regularly found along most of the Atlantic Coast. Although the striped mullet can grow to more than 15 pounds and the white mullet to about 2 pounds, much smaller immature specimens are used for bait.

These shimmering silver baitfish can be purchased fresh or frozen from seafood shops and live from bait shops. They can also be caught in a seine net in the surf at night, when the schools move close to shore to escape pursuing gamefish, or they can be snagged by drawing a treble hook through a school.

Striped bass, snook, weakfish, channel bass, tarpon, shark, sea trout and bluefish are just some of the species taken regularly on mullet.

MENHADEN This is another common baitfish that is sometimes called the bunker. The Atlantic menhaden is the particular species most often used as bait. Menhaden can be purchased and caught in the same ways as mullet, and the same species of gamefish are attracted to them.

MACKEREL Nearly two dozen species of mackerel are found in North American waters, and most species are prized as gamefish. However, they are also used as bait. Small specimens can be used whole like any other baitfish, while larger individuals can be filleted and used in pieces.

Channel bass, surfperches, croakers, weakfish, rockfish and bluefish will strike on mackerel baits.

BLOODWORMS These are also called white worms, and are generally available from most bait and tackle shops. They can be dug from mud flats during low tide along the Atlantic coast as far south as South Carolina. They also inhabit mud flats along the Pacific coast, although they are less common there. They are small, ribbed, pink worms with dark heads. A long proboscis with sharp, pinching jaws shoots out of the head when the worm is handled or otherwise threatened. Bloodworms generally exude blood when they are placed on the hook.

Striped bass, flounder, croakers, porgie, spot, tautog and surfperches are some of the species that will strike on bloodworms.

SANDWORMS These are also known as pileworms or clamworms, and are found in the same haunts as the bloodworms on the northern Atlantic coast, as far south as New Jersey, and on the Pacific coast around south and central California. They are generally found much deeper in the mud than the bloodworms. They range from dark green to black in color, with a reddish underside and many short legs along their sides.

Surfperches, flounder, croakers, corbina, tautog, porgie, stripers, weakfish, whiting and rockfish are some of the species that can be taken on sandworms.

SHRIMP The species that we commonly serve up on our dinner tables and many of the other several dozen species that are found in the coastal waters all along North America are effective bait.

Some species can be taken by net at night near low-lying lights. Others can be dug from sand or mud flats. And, of course, the largest species can be purchased fresh or frozen in seafood shops and live in bait shops.

Flounder, channel bass, halibut, surfperches,

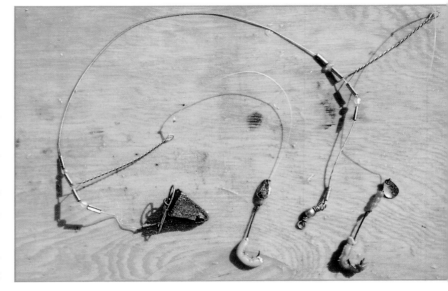

ABOVE
A two-hook bottom rig baited with bloodworms is effective on many bottom species, such as flounder.

RIGHT
Bloodworms are to saltwater as earthworms are to freshwater: the most commonly available and often-used bait there is.

TOP LEFT
Menhaden, also known as bunker, is among the most common and popular baitfish along the Atlantic coast. The species is also taken in huge quantities by commercial fishing operations.

RIGHT
A Santa Cruz, California, surf fisherman rigs bloodworms for casting.

BELOW
Most any species of shrimp, including these grass and sand shrimp, will be included in the diets of many species of gamefish and therefore make effective baits.

crustaceans are generally tan to green-brown with plated shells, legs protruding from the underside and small antennae. They are usually found buried in wet sand near the surf line along all coastlines of North America.

Sandbugs can be captured by holding a wide seine or scoop against the sand as a wave recedes. Several of the small creatures are usually used on the same hook. Striped bass, croakers, tautog, channel bass, black drum, pompano, corbina and kingfish are some of the species that will take sandbugs.

CRABS The various small crabs that can be found along almost any shoreline, both in the water and on land, are effective baits for surf fishing. Along the Atlantic coast this most often means the blue crab.

Because this species is also a much sought-after seafood, buying enough for a fishing trip can be an expensive proposition. However, the crustaceans are easily captured by using long-handled scoop nets or traps in the vegetation of shallow bays. Along the southern Atlantic coast and the Gulf of Mexico, the lady crab is easily dug from the sand in shallow water. Several species are commonly employed along various reaches of the Pacific coast.

The softshell and shedder stages of the crabs make the best baits, because without their normally hard and protective shell the crabs make a much more appealing entrée for the fish. These stages refer to the fact that crabs must shed their shells in order to grow. To use a crab that is in its hardshell version, the shell must be cracked and peeled from its back.

Striped bass, black drum, snook, channel bass and tarpon are some of the species that will take whole crabs, which should be tied to the hook instead of hooked onto it to prevent losing the bait during the cast. Kingfish, sea trout, weakfish and croakers are some of the species attracted to pieces of crab.

ABOVE LEFT
It's easy to see what this northern sea trout was feeding on just before capture: sand shrimp.

ABOVE RIGHT
Crabs, like these green crabs, are most effective when used in their softshell or shedder stages.

snook, croakers, weakfish and kingfish are some of the surf species that are attracted to shrimp.

LOBSTER This was a favorite among some of the earliest North American surf fishermen. However, the price of lobster today makes this a less popular bait. Small tails can be used like shrimp.

SANDBUGS Also called beach bugs, mole crabs, sand crabs and, incorrectly, sand fleas, these are a group of common beach fleas and amphipods related to shrimp and lobster. The small, football-shaped

CLAMS The surf clam, also called the skimmer clam, is found along sandy beaches the entire length of the Atlantic coastline. It is most often seen after being washed up into the shallows by heavy water,

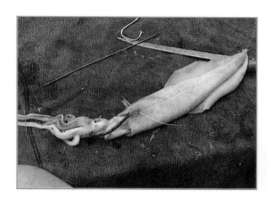

FACING PAGE, TOP
Digging for clams can be enjoyed during the slow, midday periods between surf casting.

LEFT
Squid is an effective bait for many of the species in the surf, everything from flounder to striped bass.

but it can be found during all stages of tide partly buried in the sand both on shore and underwater. Other species of clam and the several species of mussel found along both coastlines in fair abundance also make good bait.

Striped bass, black drum and channel bass are attracted to the whole clam extracted from its shell and slipped onto a hook, while fish such as the flounder, porgie, croaker and blackfish will go for pieces of the clam.

SQUIDS Many inexperienced individuals confuse squids and octopuses, envisioning the eight-tentacled monster of Jules Verne's creation for either word. With a few notable exceptions, most species of both are generally small and relatively harmless creatures. It is the squid that is commonly used as bait in surf fishing.

Fresh and frozen supplies can be purchased at most bait shops, and limited numbers can be snagged on treble hooks in the surf at night.

Whole squid and pieces will attract kingfish, porgie, striped bass, weakfish, flounder, fluke, sea bass, channel bass, cod and bluefish, among other gamefish species.

ABOVE
Keeping one eye on his rod in the sand spike, an angler works with a cast net to gather additional baitfish.

BE PREPARED

While the tackle and gear that each angler carries, beyond the few universal necessities, are a matter of personal choice, there is one rule that we all must follow: carry at least one spare of everything, or have it handy in your car. Surf fishing will definitely take its toll at some time during your angling career, and if you're not ready for the unexpected you might have to sit by and watch the hottest action of your entire lifetime pass you by. Take a tip from the Boy Scouts, "Be prepared."

TECHNIQUES

Variability is about the only constant in surf fishing: no two spots of the shoreline are exactly the same, and the same spot will throw different conditions at the angler from one day to the next. Experience and practice are the angler's primary defences against these apparent whims of the ocean.

A key essential to long-term success in surf fishing is keeping a fishing diary. Tides, fish activity, and weather influence, whilst being extremely variable from one location to the next along the shore, will generally follow something of a pattern in any one spot. It will take time, but eventually a diary that is kept up to date after each and every trip to the shore will begin to reveal the patterns for those spots that are visited regularly. To be most effective, the diary must be as detailed and specific as possible. Tides, catches, water conditions, weather conditions, lure, baits, every aspect of the trip that you can think of, should be recorded.

Veteran surf fishermen – those who you find in the same locations day-in, day-out – may offer one route to gaining experience much faster. One such angler, who is willing to share his knowledge about a particular area that you intend to fish regularly, can be a more valuable commodity than hundreds of books on the subject of surf fishing. He knows this location and speaks from personal experience.

Local bait- and tackle-shop owners can be a wealth of information about the locale that they service. However, be wary of the owner who seems more interested in loading you up with tackle than imparting knowledge. Likewise, the people who work in the local diner where the anglers hang out before and after fishing can provide valuable hints.

We all want to fish and catch something while we're waiting for the pages of the diary to fill or while we ferret out and tap the most reliable local sources of information. And, as in any fishing pursuit, there are some general standards from which any angler

can proceed. However, before accepting all of the following as "gospel," remember that every rule has its exception. And, even under optimum conditions, fish tend to feed in frenzied, short bursts rather than slowly over extended periods of time.

Tides (which will be explained in detail in a later section of this book) have the greatest impact on fishing conditions and the fish themselves. For example, high tide gives the larger fish access to feeding spots, such as coves, flats and bars, that they cannot reach during low tide. Predators make their living in the natural world by never passing up such prime opportunities. Likewise, low tide – especially

ABOVE
Even seemingly similar expanses of water will have their fish and non-fish spots. The location and success of other anglers can reveal a lot of information quickly.

LEFT
By the fall, this summer-caught, "racer" bluefish would have been several pounds heavier. Note the large head and skinny body.

filled with debris can put the fish off their feed for a few days, until it begins to clear. At that point, the fish may be even hungrier and less wary. Some excellent striped bass catches have been made along the Atlantic coast at such times, in water that is still slightly discolored.

The sun also plays an important role. In the warmer months, a good percentage of the fish move into deeper water during the time of day when the sun is at its brightest, generally the afternoon. For the same reason, overcast and stormy days often result in the best fishing throughout the day.

The smaller baitfish feel this same effect of the sun and will tend to gather close to shore during the night and at dawn and dusk. The larger gamefish generally follow the schools of baitfish, on which they depend on their daily meals.

The moon has its impact as well. It is the principal controller of our tides (which will be explained in detail later). Because of this, the period around new

the last few hours of the outgoing pull – provides a smorgasbord of baitfish being pulled along in the strong current.

For the same reason, the couple of days just after a storm has passed through an area are generally top producers in the surf. The water will be filled with the food items that the rougher waters during the storm have ripped from hiding. In addition, the larger gamefish may have ridden out a particularly rough storm in rest in deeper water, and they are now ravenous.

On the other hand, water that is too dirty, too

ABOVE
A chat with any cooperative veteran surf fisherman can make a trip to the shore much more productive.

RIGHT
Water that is too clear or too dirty can reduce fishing success.

ABOVE LEFT

Points of land that jut out into the ocean, even short distances, often provide holding spots for many species of fish.

ABOVE RIGHT

When schools are moving through an area, large catches are entirely possible.

and full moon phases – about three days before and after each – are prime times to hit the surf.

Fish themselves will often reveal the spot you should be fishing. Watch for schools of baitfish or, even better, schools of baitfish that seem to be skittering across the surface of the water. This behavior indicates that something is in pursuit of the baitfish – perhaps a whole school of the gamefish species that you seek.

Sea birds, such as gulls and terns, are a great help in spotting schools of baitfish. Just as the gamefish follow the schools from below, the birds pursue them from above. A gathering of these birds in one spot with occasional dives into the water, should be seen as a beacon attracting your lure.

Wherever a river empties into the ocean or an inlet draws ocean water inland is a prime location. At these spots gamefish will find plenty of structure and bountiful baitfish. In addition, the mixing of fresh and salt water at these locations is favored by some species of gamefish.

SHORES

≈

Most shore environments can be classified as one of three categories: rocky shore, sandy beach or jetty.

ROCKY SHORES These tend to present the type of underwater structure that attracts and holds healthy populations of baitfish and the many other items that gamefish include in their diet. Pockets, drop-offs and small canyon-like openings abound throughout these areas.

They often can be spotted from nearby, elevated dunes and cliffs, or by watching for the spots where waves are breaking. At the same time, these areas often offer the angler a ready means to wading relatively close to deeper water, which can then be reached with shorter, less taxing casts.

ABOVE
High vantage points can help the angler to spot likely locations of his quarry.

≈

LEFT
Steep, rocky drop-offs, such as this rocky spot near Santa Cruz, California, often prove highly attractive to many species of fish.

≈

Storms have less of an impact on these areas than on sandy beaches over the years, resulting in less change to the shore. As fish are highly opportunistic creatures, the same spot that produced a member of a certain species on one day may well produce a similar fish a few days later and another a few days after that. Anglers who have fished a specific rocky shore for several years can often point to individual rocks and ledges that have produced fish regularly.

Tall boulders or high ledges that rise directly above these areas offer the unique opportunity to drop bait-rigs straight down into likely-looking, deeper pockets to avoid the snags that are so common when fishing here. Rocky areas tend to take a heavier toll on fishing tackle, something that the angler must resign himself to if he wants to access

LEFT

Flyfishing is effective on many species, including this striped bass taken along a rocky shoreline.

BELOW

Just about any obstruction jutting out into the ocean will have nearly magical fish-attracting powers.

the fish that they harbor. Surface- or shallow-running artificial lures are good choices, as are flies. Weights might be replaced with small, cloth sacks filled with pebbles that can be lost with less frustration.

SANDY BEACHES These are the areas where most of North America's surf fishing is done, and don't usually present the problems of snags and hang-ups. However they also are not nearly as easy to "read" as the rocky shore areas. Long stretches that hold very few fish might look relatively no different from those spots that abound with life.

Watching schools of baitfish, or the sea birds that follow them, generally will lead the angler to gamefish. Exploration casting is another quick way to get to know a particular stretch of beach. Walking along the beach, the angler stops and makes two or three casts at one spot. If he gets a strike or some other indication that this is a "fishy" spot, he continues to fish here. On the other hand, if he receives no

clues in the first two or three casts, he moves another 20 yards or so down the beach and casts another two or three times. If he connects he continues to fish here; if not he moves on down the beach. A couple miles of beach can be covered quickly in this manner, which is repeated on the return to the starting point. The angler should be storing all possible information from this exploration to be recorded later in his diary.

On most beaches, waves that break at some distance offshore generally reveal the location of bars or the fact that the beach slopes gently for quite a distance. Usually the first curl of the waves indicates the drop-off point, where gamefish will be feeding. This first line of breakers should be fished heavily. In addition, offshore bars usually offer deeper gullies through themselves, where the current is stronger and pulls a concentrated selection of baitfish and other food items through.

Waves that break almost at the shoreline indicate a much more steeply sloping beach, where fish will often chase the lure almost right up onto the beach.

TOP

The surf zone offers the angler many non-hook-and-line opportunities, such as smelt fishing with a cast net.

≈

CENTER

Many surf anglers focus on casting as far toward the horizon as they possibly can, but the surf right at our feet should never be overlooked entirely.

≈

TECHNIQUES

43

BELOW

Even a quick look at this fish-attracting spot reveals it as a likely location to cast a line.

≈

The relative lightness and darkness of the water is likewise revealing of underwater conditions. Lighter water, when conditions are calm, generally indicates shallow water. Darker water under the same conditions reveals the holes, drop-offs and channels. Such darker areas tend to be gathering spots for baitfish and thus for larger gamefish.

Surveying the beach and surf from a nearby, elevated dune or cliff will also reveal many of these characteristics, as well as large schools of baitfish.

Baitfishing on sandy beaches can be quite productive. Keeping the bait on or near the bottom, where the fish expect to find most meals, is crucial.

JETTIES (BREAKWATERS) These are defined as manmade structures – usually rock and concrete – that have been built out into the water to protect a harbor or shoreline by changing water current and tide directions. A more practical definition for the surf fisherman is simply "fish magnets." The baitfish and shellfish that gamefish eat tend to congregate in large numbers around these structures, drawing the fish into easy casting range.

The jetties have the added advantage, from the angler's perspective, of offering ready access to deeper water. Some of these structures extend a mile or more out into the water. Wooden and moss/slime-covered surfaces, however, present the danger of slipping that must be kept constantly in mind.

Additionally, these structures can be crowded on weekends and holidays, forcing shoulder-to-shoulder conditions that many anglers find objectionable.

Weekdays, however, generally present less crowded conditions that allow a lone fisherman or a few anglers to probe the entire length of the jetty. On sunny days, an effective tactic is to begin fishing in the early morning near the shore and moving toward the ocean as the sun creeps higher.

"Buddy" fishing is advisable on jetties, where one slip can toss an angler into quite deep water. A long-handled gaff will make landing a much easier and safer task on these structures.

FORMATION OF TIDES

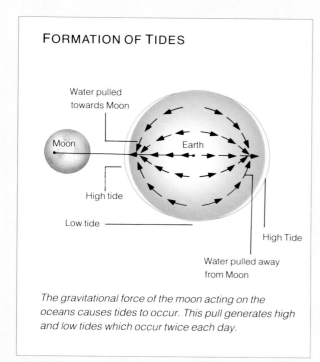

The gravitational force of the moon acting on the oceans causes tides to occur. This pull generates high and low tides which occur twice each day.

SPRING TIDES AND NEAP TIDES

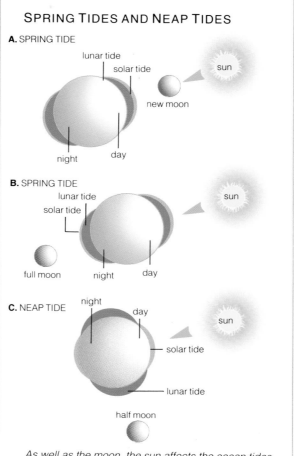

As well as the moon, the sun affects the ocean tides. The highest and lowest spring tides happen when the sun, moon and earth are directly aligned with each other. When a right angle is formed between the sun, earth and moon, the neap tides occur – that is, the lowest tidal range.

Oceans cover just over 70 per cent of the Earth's surface. There are 140 million square miles of ocean surface, covering an estimated 322 million cubic miles of water, by volume. But for the purposes of this book, we're concerned with only those few hundred yards of the North American coast where ocean meets land – the surf.

On a rough twelve-hour rotation all ocean waters on the face of the Earth rise and fall. These tides, as we have come to call them, are one effect of the gravitational pull of the moon and the sun on the Earth and the water. Because the moon is much closer to the Earth, it exerts the greatest influence over our tides. When the moon is directly above a point of water on the Earth, it pulls on that spot of water, which then rises above its normal level. A similar pull is being exerted on the spot of the Earth exactly opposite the first spot. High tide is thus occurring at both these spots. At the same time, spots perpendicular across the Earth from each of our first two spots are experiencing low tides.

The moon circles the Earth at a rate of slightly more than 24 hours per complete circle. Because of this each spot of water experiences two high tides and two low tides every day.

Meanwhile, the sun has a similar, although lesser impact on our waters.

When the sun, moon and Earth fall into a direct line – at new and full moon – the solar and lunar effects on the water coincide, resulting in higher high tides and lower low tides. These are often referred to as spring tides. By the same natural principles, when the moon and sun are at right angles to one another (relative to the Earth) – when the moon is in its first and third quarters – the solar and lunar effects are opposing one another. The high tides are then lower than normal and the low tides are higher than normal. These periods are referred to as neap tides.

The spring and neap tides do not occur exactly on the phase of the moon, but generally about 60 hours afterwards.

The greatest high tides on Earth are found in the Bay of Fundy, between Nova Scotia and New Brunswick, Canada. Here the difference between high tide and low tide has been measured at more than 60 feet.

With the rising and falling of the tides, the oceans experience tidal currents. These currents are actually regular horizontal movements across the waters. The cycle of these currents is just over 6 hours. For example, for the 6 hours plus a few minutes of high tide the current flows shoreward. Then it reverses and for roughly the same amount of time flows away from shore.

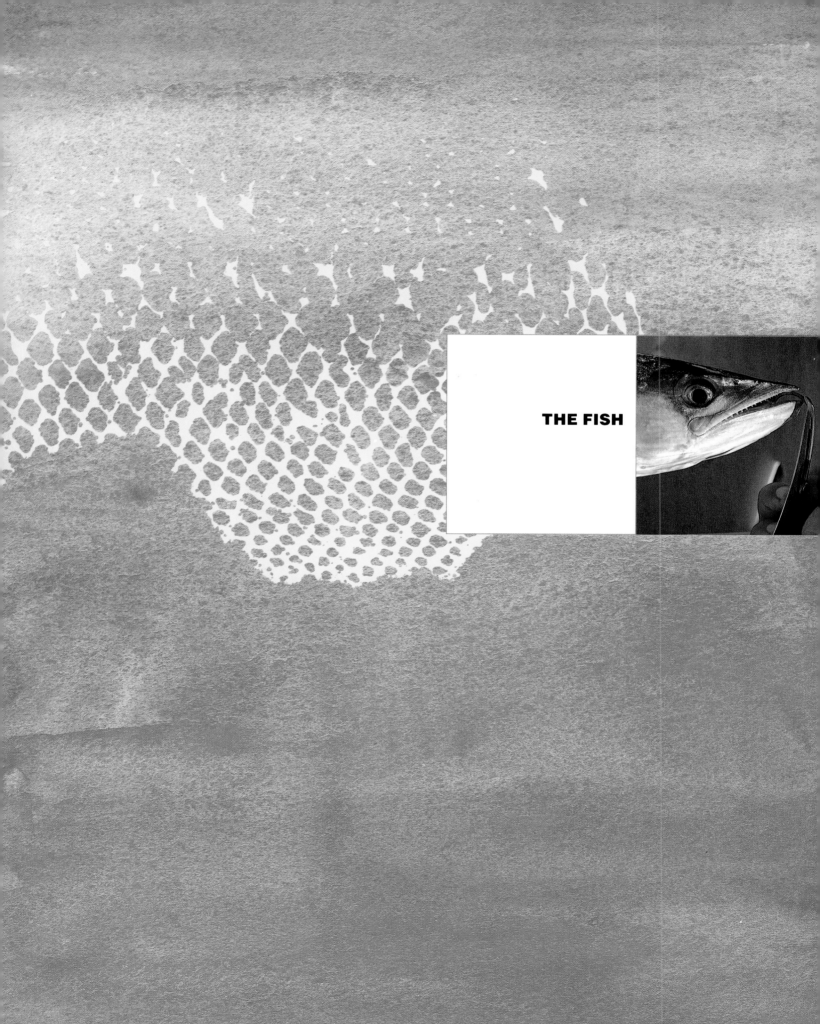

THE FISH

An almost unbelievable array of fish species inhabit the surf waters along the North American coast at one time or another during the year. Many are taken by anglers; however, the following discussion has to be restricted to some of the most commonly caught and popular species.

STRIPED BASS

Morone saxatilis

This is the earliest recorded surf-fishing catch in North America, although the native Americans were probably fishing many other species as well long before the Europeans arrived and began casting for stripers. The species has been the most popular of Atlantic coast surf fish ever since.

It is also known as the rockfish, greenhound and squidhound in certain localities within its widespread range. The fish is dark green to nearly black on its back, silver on its sides, with several horizontal rows of closely arranged black dots and white on its underside.

BLUEFISH

Pomatomus saltatrix

This was long considered a trash fish during the early, more exclusive days of surf fishing, as were most species other than the highly prized striped bass. With the growth in popularity of the sport in more recent years, however, the bluefish has gained much favor.

Well-deserving of this newfound favor, the bluefish is a great fighter, offering everything from flailing leaps out of the water to long, powerful runs. It takes an extremely wide variety of baits and lures, in manners ranging from the gentlest of nibbles to rod-jolting slashes.

The only member of its family, the bluefish is bluish green on its back and partly down its sides, fading to white on its underside. It inhabits the

Atlantic coast, with larger specimens generally steering clear of inshore waters except during the spring and fall migrations. A maximum weight for this species stands at about 40 to 50 pounds.

Bluefish of nearly the same size tend to travel together in schools. This is because the fish is so highly predatory as to be cannibalistic on smaller specimens of its own kind. As an efficient predator, the bluefish is equipped with an impressive set of choppers that experienced anglers know to respect, even after the fish has been gaffed.

ABOVE
Striped bass

LEFT

A look at the teeth of a
bluefish quickly reveals
how the fish got the
nickname of chopper.

≈

ABOVE LEFT
An angler beaches a nice
bluefish.

≈

ABOVE RIGHT
Bluefish

≈

LEFT
Striped bass remain one of
the most popular saltwater
species along the Atlantic
coast.

≈

SPOTTED SEATROUT

Cynoscion nebulosus

Along the southern Atlantic coast and in the Gulf of Mexico, the spotted seatrout is among the most popular of surf fish. It is readily taken on flashy artificials and live bait, with shrimp and needlefish as favored food items.

The fish is gray to silver on its back and partly down its sides, with scattered black dots throughout this area and in the dorsal and caudal fins. Its underside is silver.

Several massive kills of the spotted seatrout have been recorded over the years, attributed to the impacts of sudden cold temperatures.

SUMMER FLOUNDER

Paralichthys dentatus

Also known as the fluke, this is a very popular surf
and party boat fish, although it is not a strong fighter.
Good catches are also taken from jetties and bridges.
An inhabitant of the Atlantic coast from Maine to
North Carolina, it keeps mainly to the bottom or
very close to it.

Coloring ranges from gray to olive with a reddish
tint and large, irregular spots along the upper side,
and a pale underside. Average weight is 2 to 6
pounds; maximum is about 30 pounds.

Small fish, pieces of larger fish, squids and artificial lures worked near the bottom are best bets for
this species.

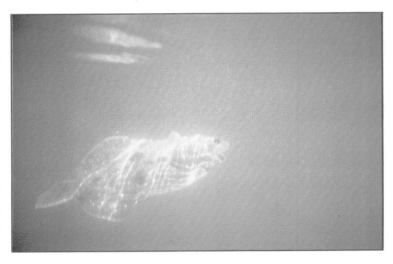

SOUTHERN FLOUNDER

Paralichthys lethostigma

A closely related species, the southern flounder
generally replaces the summer flounder from south
of South Carolina and in the Gulf of Mexico. It is a
slightly smaller bottom fish, averaging 1 to 3 pounds,
with large specimens at 15 to 20 pounds. The southern flounder also lacks the summer flounder's distinct spots along the upperside of the body.

The species shows a decided preference for those
areas where salt water and fresh water mix, resulting in reduced salinity. It has also been found in
considerable numbers well upriver into the freshwater zone. Small fish make up the bulk of its diet.

WINTER FLOUNDER

Pseudopleuronectes americanus

While summer and southern flounders are members
of the left-eye family, the winter flounder belongs
to the right-eye family. This means that both of its
eyes are on the right side of its body. It goes by
many localized names, including black flounder,
flatfish, blueback and muddab.

A resident of the Atlantic coast as far south as Georgia, the winter flounder varies from reddish brown to gray. Average specimens weigh 1 to 3 pounds, while the fish reaches its maximum growth at about 6 pounds.

The winter flounder constantly moves throughout its territory in search of food, mainly small fish. Large specimens can be found in the surf year-round, although more of them seem to appear there in fall. The species has been found in estuaries, near to the freshwater zone.

ROCK SOLE

Lepidopsetta billineata

This is another right-eyed flounder. It ranges along the Pacific coast from southern California north, generally inhabiting gravel bottom areas. It is brown with darker brown spots and occasionally a red tint. Maximum weight is about 5 pounds, while the average is 1 to 2 pounds. Crustaceans, mollusks and sea worms form the bulk of its diet.

DIAMOND TURBOT

Hypsopsetta guttula

Another Pacific right-eye, this is a common species of the quiet coastal waters, bays and sloughs of the California coast. Large numbers are taken every year on pieces of clam, shrimp and ghost shrimp. Although the fish grows to no more than 4 pounds, it can put up a considerable fight on light tackle.

STARRY FLOUNDER

Platichthys stellatus

Even more widespread, this Pacific coast species occurs commonly from Santa Barbara, California, north to northern Alaska. Although catches of more than 20 pounds have been reported, the average is about 2 pounds. The species is the most common flatfish available in northern California waters.

ATLANTIC COD

Gadus morhua

This is a fish of the cold water, ranging along the Atlantic coast as far south as North Carolina. It occurs in two color phases, red and gray, and has been recorded at more than 200 pounds. The average specimen taken is between 10 and 15 pounds, but fish up to 70 pounds are not uncommon.

Larger specimens tend to keep to deeper water, except when the cold of winter allows them to move into the inshore waters. Jetty fishing for cod will prove productive throughout the year. The diet of the Atlantic cod is quite varied, including squids, fish, crustaceans and mollusks.

GRAY SNAPPER

Lutjanus griseus

This is the most common member of the snapper family in the Atlantic ocean. It ranges from New York south into the Gulf of Mexico. It is gray along its back and sides, somewhat paler on its underside with a reddish tint.

Large gray snappers – slightly more than 10 pounds in weight – are extremely wary of anything that appears even the slightest bit unnatural, such as artificial lures and baited hooks. Successful anglers take these tasty fish by rigging live shrimp on small hooks at the ends of the most invisible leaders they can find.

THE SCHOOLMASTER

Lutjanus apodus

One of the smallest of the snappers, the schoolmaster averages less than 1 pound, although some 5-pounders have been reported. This resident of the southern Atlantic is yellow with darker vertical lines across its sides. It generally stays close to rocky structures, where it finds protection. Bait and artificial lures are effective.

LANE SNAPPER

Lutjanus synagris

An equally small snapper this is also of the southern Atlantic coast. Most specimens of this vertically red-and-yellow-striped fish average less than 1 pound in weight. On the other hand, the species offers extremely tasty flesh and ready availability under nearly all surf conditions. It hits a wide array of live and dead bait as well as many artificial lures.

CUBERA SNAPPER

Lutjanus cyanopterus

Also known as the Cuban snapper, this is the largest member of the snapper family, growing to more than 100 pounds. It too inhabits the southern Atlantic coast, where it is generally found near underwater ledges. The fish is green to gray on its back and sides, and pale green on the underside, with dark red eyes. Bait and artificial lures will tempt this strong-fighting species.

DOG SNAPPER

Lutjanus jocu

Rocky areas around the southern Florida coastline are home to the dog snapper, which can grow to more than 20 pounds but generally is less than 5 pounds. The fish's sides are patterned in alternating darker and lighter shades of green with a reddish tint on the underside and reddish brown fins.

LADYFISH

Elops saurus

This fish includes "10-pounder" among its common aliases, but this nickname is far from appropriate as the fish rarely exceeds 6 pounds in weight. What the ladyfish lacks in size, however, it makes up in spunk. A battle with this species on light tackle, complete with lots of acrobatics above the water, is something the angler will remember.

In addition, the ladyfish tends to travel in large, hungry schools and a lure drawn through such a school will draw several fast strikes until one of the fish is finally hooked.

Also called the chino, this species is common along the Atlantic coast from South Carolina south. Schools of the green to blue-backed, silver-sided fish are often found in protected bays and estuaries.

BELOW
Ladyfish

KINGFISH

Menticurrhus spp.

Four species of this fish inhabit the Atlantic coast and the Gulf of Mexico. They are all bottom feeders, with diets consisting mainly of mollusks, crabs and shrimps. They are generally small – less than 1 foot in length – but make tasty panfish.

LEFT
Kingfish

WEAKFISH

Cynoscion regalis

This fish was given its name in condemnatory deference to the extremely delicate nature of its mouth. Hooks can be torn from this thin flesh with the slightest jerk of a line.

Also known as the yellowfin and the gray weakfish, this species is olive green along its back, green to blue with a golden sheen and scattered dark spots on its sides, and a silvery underside. The fins show a yellowish tint.

It inhabits the Atlantic coastline from Massachusetts south, and will enter inlets and estuaries as far as the freshwater line. The weakfish is generally found in schools and several can often be taken before a school moves off. A maximum of 18 pounds is achieved by very few specimens, with most falling between 8 and 10 pounds. Fish, crabs, squids, eels, shrimps and aquatic worms are all taken.

WHITE SEA BASS

Cynoscion nobilis

This is found along the Pacific coast of the United States, although much more commonly along the southern half of California. Reaching weights up to 80 pounds, with an average of less than 40 pounds, the fish is gray to blue-gray across its back, silver on its sides and white on the underside.

It is often taken near kelp beds, where it feeds on squids, fish and crustaceans. The white sea bass will take a variety of baits and artificial lures that are fished slowly and near the bottom.

BLACK SEA BASS

Centropristis striata

A fish more often associated with boat fishing over wrecks and other structures, but at certain times of the year – primarily in the spring – it does move to inshore waters. Some individuals will remain in the shallower waters into late fall, while others will move back out much sooner.

The gray-brown to blue-black fish ranges along the Atlantic coast from Massachusetts south, showing a definite preference for hard, rocky bottom areas with clear water. The average black sea bass weighs about 2 pounds, while the maximum is about 7 pounds.

BLACK DRUM

Pognias cromis

Like the black sea bass, this is generally a species of the offshore waters of the Atlantic from Maine south and the Gulf of Mexico. But each spring a run of the fish from Delaware to the Carolinas brings the larger specimens within surf-casting range.

A bottom fish, the black drum makes its diet primarily of crustaceans and mollusks. The same items are generally used for bait for this strong fighter. Average specimens range to 40 pounds, while trophy individuals may tip the scales at 150 pounds. It is a shimmering silver fish, with black fins.

RED DRUM

Sciaenops ocellata

This inhabits much the same water as the black drum. It is also known as the channel bass and redfish. Specimens of more than 90 pounds have been taken on rod and reel, although the average is closer to 50 pounds or less. The fish is bronze to copper colored with one or more black spots at the base of its tail.

It is a bottom feeder, primarily eating crustaceans and mollusks, but can be taken on live baits ranging from bloodworms and sandbugs to its more conventional diet, and on a variety of artificial lures.

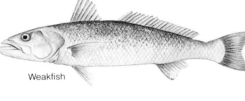

Weakfish

ABOVE
These red drum were taken
on mullet pieces as bait.

TAUTOG

Tautoga onitis

Also called the blackfish, this fish is well adapted to its diet of crustaceans and mollusks, with a set of thick, blunt, crushing teeth. A resident of the Atlantic coast, this bottom feeder moves about widely within its territory and populations tend to do the same within much larger areas. The species averages 3 pounds in weight, although large specimens have tipped the scales at 30 pounds.

FRENCH GRUNT

Haemulon flavolineatum

Southern Atlantic waters are home for this small, but abundant fish. It averages less than 1 pound in weight, but is a top-notch panfish. It is marked with horizontal bars of orange-brown and green-blue and an extremely large, black eye. Shrimp and cut baitfish make excellent bait for the French grunt.

JEWFISH

Epinephelus itajara

This is among the largest species to be found in inshore waters. Ledges and holes close to shore or near bridges or piers are the favored haunts of this largest member of the grouper family. It occurs primarily in the southern Atlantic and is rather common in and around southern Florida. The fish is marked with irregular bars and stripes on its sides.

Although a few can reach a weight of 700 pounds, it is not much of a fighter. When hooked, the jewfish simply bulls its way back into its hiding places, from which the angler must work to remove it. It will take both bait and artificial lures. The flesh is extremely tasty.

SPOTFIN CROAKER

Roncador stearnsi

This is a popular surf species along the southern California coast, with the most productive fishing coming in the late summer months with live baits such as clams, crabs or pileworms.

The fish is gray to silver with one large black spot at the base of each pectoral fin and a nearly white underside. It reaches a maximum weight of about 9 pounds and tends to gather in holes and under ledges just beyond the breakers.

WHITE CROAKER

Genyonemus lineatus

One of five members of the croaker family found along the California coast, it is generally so eager to take any bait offered to it that many anglers consider it a pest species. It grows to about 1 to 1½ pounds.

OCEAN PERCH

Sebastes marinus

Also called the rosefish, red perch and sea perch, the ocean perch is the only Atlantic coast member of the rockfish family. It grows to more than 5 pounds, but the average specimen is about 1 pound.

SURFPERCH FAMILY

Embiotocidae

This is a large group of Pacific coast fish that inhabit both inshore and offshore waters. Common names often reveal their habitat preferences: surfperch generally inhabit the surf, sea perch are more offshore-oriented and the habitat of the perch varies considerably.

BARRED SURFPERCH *Amphistichus argentens* This fish forms the basis of surf fishing along the central and southern California coast. Olive in color with darker vertical bars and spots on its sides, the species grows to about 5 pounds. Sandcrabs are a favored food item and a popular bait for this fish.

CALICO SURFPERCH *Amphistichus koelzi* A close relative of the barred surfperch, which it also closely

ABOVE
Surfperch

≈

resembles. The principal difference lies in the fact that the calico is found in more northerly waters along the California coast.

WALLEYE SURFPERCH *Hyperprosopon argenteum* Inhabiting the same general range as both of these species, the walleye surfperch is probably the second most taken fish in the California surf. It grows to about 3 or slightly more pounds and is gray-blue with indistinct darker bars running down its sides.

SILVER SURFPERCH *Hyperprosopon ellipticum* Similar to the walleye surfperch, although with a more silvery color, the silver surfperch inhabits a larger range, from Washington to southern California.

REDTAIL SURFPERCH *Amphistichus rhodoterus* Another close relative of the barred surfperch, this is fish also known as the porgy. Sandy beaches from Washington to central California generally play host to this species.

RUBBERLIP SEA PERCH *Rhacochilus toxotes* This is among the best eating of the surfperches. Its common name is derived from its thick, protruding lips. It is white with a tint of blue-black that is more pronounced on its lower sides and underside, and grows to about 5 pounds. The southern half of the California coast is its home.

RAINBOW SEA PERCH *Hypsurus caryi* One of the most colorful of the surfperch family, with distinct horizontal strips of blue, red and orange across its body; streaks of blue across its orange head; and orange fins. It ranges along the entire California coast and grows to a couple pounds.

WHITE SEA PERCH *Phanerodon furcatus* Occupying sandy areas along much of the Pacific coast, as far north as Canada, the white sea perch grows to about 3 or 4 pounds. It is silvery colored, darker on its back and tail.

BLACK SEA PERCH *Embiotoca jacksoni* Rocky areas, natural and manmade, are the favorite haunts of the black perch, which ranges along the central and southern California coast. The fish is brown, tinted with many other color variations, and grows to about 4 pounds.

SHINER PERCH *Cymatogaster aggregate* A small but abundant surfperch that occurs along all but the northernmost Pacific coast. Large specimens of this species weigh 1 pound at most. The fish is green along its back and upper sides, and silvery along its lower sides and underside, with three vertical bands of yellow along its sides.

OPALEYE

Girella nigricans

Named for its large, opal-like eye, this fish inhabits the coastal waters of California, usually over rocky bottoms or near kelp beds. It is also known as the blue-eyed perch, blue bass, button perch and Catalina perch.

The light green to green-blue fish, with a darker lateral line, is a popular quarry with surf fishermen in the winter, when the larger specimens (up to 15 pounds) move into inshore waters. Baits include various mollusks and shrimps.

SKIPJACK TUNA

Euthynnus pelamis

This fish inhabits the Atlantic from Massachusetts south. The average catch is from 5 to 15 pounds, with a maximum of about 50 pounds. A very prolific breeder, the skipjack is the most widespread member of the tuna family and often travels in large schools. It is a shimmering blue along its back, fading into gray and then into off-white with several distinct horizontal lines. The skipjack is taken on many baits and artificial lures, although feathers are a top producer.

LEFT
Skipjack tuna

ABOVE
Skipjack

BONITO FAMILY

Sarda spp.

Closely related to the tuna family, representatives of the bonito are found on both coasts.

ATLANTIC BONITO *Sarda sarda* This can be found from Maine south to Maryland. It can grow to nearly 20 pounds, although most specimens are between 3 and 8 pounds. Artificial lures retrieved swiftly are likely to produce good catches of this fine-fighting, good-eating fish.

PACIFIC BONITO *Sarda chiliensis* Quite a similar fish within its range along from British Columbia south to California. It is also known as the California bonita.

STRIPED BONITO *Sarda orientalis* This is a bit smaller and occupies a more southerly Pacific range that includes southern California waters.

TARPON

Megalops atlantica

The tarpon can grow to be quite large – up to 8 feet in length and 350 pounds in weight – but only after many years of life. Closer-to-average 100-pounders have been aged at about 15 years. The fish's normal range extends along the Atlantic coast from North Carolina south, although it has been taken as far north as Canadian waters.

A much sought-after gamefish, the tarpon is blue to dark green on its back and shimmering silver on its sides and underside. Its trademark is the bull-dog-like face with protruding lower jaw. The species appears particularly drawn to areas of lower water salinity, such as the mouths of rivers and estuaries.

It is a legendary gamefish, proving to be both wary before the hooking and a strong fighter capable of terrific leaps and powerful runs after the hook is set. Live bait, selected from the fish's large diet that includes crabs, mullet and catfish, and an assortment of artificial lures are employed successfully against the fish.

SHARKS

Squaliformes spp.

These carry a great deal of excitement for many people, probably more attributable to the myth that surrounds them than any scientific facts.

SMOOTH DOGFISH *Mustelus canis* One of the most common shark species in United States coastal waters, the smooth dogfish ranges along the Atlantic coast from Massachusetts south and throughout the Gulf of Mexico. The slender, gray-to-brown shark averages about 2 feet in length, although specimens as long as 5 feet have been taken. It eats fish, squids, crabs and lobsters, and occasionally travels upriver into freshwater areas.

BROWN SHARK *Carcharhinus milberti* Just as common in inshore waters of the Atlantic from Massachusetts to Florida is the brown or sandbar shark. It averages from 30 to 100 pounds, although specimens nearing 200 pounds have been taken.

SAND TIGER *Odontaspis taurus* Although this shark may grow to more than 250 pounds, most specimens are caught in shallow water, usually less than 10 feet deep. Also known as the sand shark, the fish inhabits the entire Atlantic coast of the United States. The sand tiger is gray-brown with irregular yellowish spots across its midsection and posterior.

Generally a surf species of the warmer months, the sand tiger has been found upriver as far as the freshwater point. It is a rather lazy species, eating a diet that consists primarily of squids, crabs and fish.

SCALLOPED HAMMERHEAD *Sphyrna lervini* This shark grows to a maximum of about 12 feet and is a resident of the Atlantic coast from New Jersey south.

SMOOTH HAMMERHEAD *Sphyrna zygaena* This might reach a length of more than 14 feet and weighs nearly 900 pounds, although most specimens are about half that size. It lives along the Atlantic coast and the Gulf of Mexico, making annual summertime migrations northward. The smooth hammerhead is often taken in very shallow water.

GREAT HAMMERHEAD *Sphyrna mokarran* This shark can be as long as 18 feet. It inhabits a much more restricted range along the Atlantic coast, from North Carolina south.

BONNETHEAD SHARK *Sphyrna tiburo* The hammer is replaced with a shovel-like shape for a head, making the bonnethead an equally identifiable species. Gray-brown in color, paler on its underside, it can grow to more than 6 feet in length. The average, however, is close to 3 or 4 feet.

The bonnethead shark occupies a range along the Atlantic coast from Maine south, but is most com-

ABOVE

Hammerhead shark

TOP LEFT

Sharks commonly feed along calm beaches during ebb tide.

TOP RIGHT

Mako shark

mon south of North Carolina and in the Gulf of Mexico. Within that smaller range, it is one of the most commonly encountered sharks in the surf.

DUSKY SHARK *Carcharhinus obscurus* Although less common than the very similar sandbar shark, the dusky shark is much larger, reaching weights of more than 600 pounds. It is one of the largest species regularly found in the Atlantic surf, although it is more often an offshore fish.

MAKO SHARK *Isurus oxyrinchus* This is the classic shark, with its bright blue back and creamy white sides and underside. It is also the most sought-after of all sharks. Along the Atlantic coast, the species ranges as far north as Cape Cod; along the Pacific Coast, as far north as northern California.

It is one of the greatest fighting fish in the ocean, able to deliver reel-singing runs and water-clearing leaps. Average specimens range from 50 to 200 pounds, while individuals of more than 1,000 pounds have been taken with some regularity. It is most commonly an offshore species, although it is

taken in shallow water in the mid-Atlantic region.

BULL SHARK *Carcharhinus leucas* A non-stop feeding machine, the bull shark eats nearly anything that crosses its path. The gray to gray-brown shark, with a white underside, grows to more than 10 feet and 400 pounds, but most specimens taken in the surf are between 6 and 7 feet. It is a common, shallow-water species of the Atlantic, from North Carolina south, and the Gulf of Mexico.

BLUE SHARK *Prionace glauca* Although this is far from one of the best fighting surf species, it is one of our most colorful sharks. Bright sky-blue sides, accented by a snow-white underside, give the fish an almost cartoon-like appearance. Specimens of more than 400 pounds have been caught, although 50 to 200 pounds is much more common.

An inhabitant of both the Atlantic and Pacific coasts, the blue shark often travels in packs for foraging and scavenging. It will eat just about anything organic and some things that are not, although the bulk of its diet is made up of fish, squids and

THE MYSTIQUE OF
THE SHARK

Of all the considerable creatures in the oceans, sharks stand out as a perceived threat to man. They have justifiably been described as the ultimate killing/eating machines, conjuring even more images of death and destruction.

They have given rise to writings such as this passage from *20,000 Leagues under the Sea* by Jules Verne: "If you were asked to hunt the lion in the plains of Atlas, or the tiger in the Indian jungles, what would you say? Ha! Ha! It seems we are going to hunt the tiger or the lion. But when you are invited to hunt the shark in its natural element, you would perhaps reflect before accepting the invitation."

Like few other creatures, the shark is planted in our psyche.

We fear this fish. The first time you drag one onto the beach, after a long and tiring battle in the surf, and a crowd gathers round the fish, you'll get the full measure of how much fear the shark can generate.

The common image is a streamlined, pointed-nose fish with a tall dorsal fin slicing the surface of the water as it bears down on us with a gaping maw filled with razor-edged teeth. This is certainly one description of sharks, or at least of some species of shark.

But in reality there are about 300 different species swimming through the oceans of the world today, and many are quite different in appearance and expected actions.

sea birds. The species is not very wary, and individual fish are often hooked again immediately after being released.

LEMON SHARK *Negaprion brevirostris* This is a much better fighter. The yellow-brown fish grows to no more than 11 feet and is common along the Atlantic coast, from North Carolina south, and in the Gulf of Mexico. It offers top-notch fighting ability and will actively chase all sorts of artificial lures and flies.

LEOPARD SHARK *Triatis semifasciata* A distinctly marked species, the leopard shark sports a gray skin crossed with a dozen darker bands on its back, and irregular, scattered spots along its sides. A common Pacific coast species, from Oregon to southern California, the leopard shark generally reaches a maximum length of no more than 5 feet. However, it is a much sought-after species for its great fighting ability and excellent taste.

TIGER SHARK *Galeocerdo cuvieri* The young sometimes bear a resemblance to the leopard shark, with darker stripes along their back and sides. The adult tiger shark, however, generally loses these markings in favor of an overall gray-brown coloring.

It would be difficult to name anything, alive or dead, that the tiger shark does not eat or try to eat, including man. It is one of the species often involved in attacks on humans. Although it is a large shark – it can reach 18 feet and 2,000 pounds, although the average is about 13 feet and 900 to 1,000 pounds – the fish is taken with some regularity in the inshore waters along the Atlantic coast from Virginia south and in the Gulf of Mexico. It is a lazy shark and not much of a fighter.

STINGRAY FAMILY

Dasyatidae

Closely related to the sharks are the members of the stingray family. Although there is wide variation, these fish are usually flat with a diamond or circular shape to their bodies and pointed tails. They are mostly small, but specimens have been taken at 14 feet in length and weighing hundreds of pounds.

SHOVELNOSE GUITARFISH

Rhinobatos productus

This is found over sand or mud bottoms from central California through the Gulf of California. It grows to about 4 feet, but is not much of a gamefish and is generally considered a pest by surf fishermen.

ATLANTIC GUITARFISH

Rhinobatos lentiginosus

A close relative of the shovelnose guitarfish, this is much smaller (maximum to about 2½ feet) and is regarded in the same way by surf fishermen.

LEFT
Stingray
≈

SHEEPSHEAD

Archosargus probatocephalus

The Atlantic Ocean, Pacific Ocean and the Gulf of Mexico each hold a subspecies of the sheepshead in healthy numbers. However the fish, also known as the convict fish because of the half-dozen or so vertical bars that run down its silvery sides, is a difficult species to get onto the hook. Rarely will it strike at an artificial lure, and it remains wary even when responding to a chum of crushed fiddler crabs, one of its favorite food items. Other crabs, shrimps and sandbugs are also used for bait with some success. Specimens of this good-eating fish average about 2 feet, although some of more than 3 feet have been taken.

SMALLTOOTH SAWFISH

Pristis pectinata

This can be found throughout the Gulf of Mexico and along the Atlantic coast, as far north as New York during the summer. But, as the waters cool each fall, its range shrinks to Florida and south.

The fish takes its name from its thin, tooth-lined snout that looks remarkably like the blade of a chainsaw. It uses this beak to attack its prey fish in a sideways slashing motion, aiming to maim and cripple individual fish for later consumption. Because of this strange feeding habit, cut-up baitfish cast into a school of fish under attack makes an excellent bait.

Smalltooth sawfish have been caught that measured more than 18 feet, but a 16-footer that weighs about 700 pounds is generally considered a large specimen of this fish.

ATLANTIC MACKEREL

Scomber scombrusa

This is found all along the Atlantic coast, ranging up to a maximum weight of 35 pounds. It is blue to green with darker vertical bars along the upper half of its sides and a silver underside.

GAFFTOPSAIL CATFISH

Bagre marinus

This is a bottom fish that occurs along the Atlantic coast from Massachusetts south, although it is rarely found in the surf during the winter in the northern part of its range. It spends these colder months in deeper waters to avoid the cold.

The fish is gray to blue on its sides, darker on its back and paler on its underside, with irregular darker dots along the lateral line and touches of orange-brown at the edges of its fins. The dorsal and pectoral fins are noticeably elongated, resembling the sails of a ship. Rarely will the gafftopsail catfish reach a length of more than 2 feet or a weight of more than 5 pounds.

Most specimens are taken with bait fished on the bottom, but the fish will strike artificials on occasion. Its flesh has a pleasant taste.

Sheepshead

LEFT	RIGHT
Mackerel	Gafftopsail catfish

NEEDLEFISH FAMILY

Belonidae

This is a group of related, small fish with the namesake, needle-like, long and thin beaks. The family is represented along both the Atlantic and Pacific coasts and in the Gulf of Mexico. Its largest representative is the houndfish, which grows to about 5 feet in length in the Pacific, while the most common member is the smaller Atlantic needlefish. All members of the family eagerly attack artificial lures of all descriptions, as well as live bait.

GRASS PORGY

Calamus arctifons

Commonly found in thick patches of vegetation throughout the Gulf of Mexico, this fish is olive in color with scattered white spots, and yellow spots along the lateral line. The fish grows to only a foot in length, and shrimp and pieces of fish are the most productive baits. The flesh is quite edible.

SCUP

Stenotomus chrysops

This is also known as the porgy in the waters it inhabits along the Atlantic coast and the Gulf of Mexico. Silver, with a distinctly darker horizontal line along its sides, the scup reaches a maximum length of about 20 inches and a weight of up to 4 pounds. Baits fished on the bottom will take the fish, which makes good table fare.

SARGO

Anisotremus davidsonii

A common member of the grunt family, this fish is metallic silver with a gray tint on the back. It is marked with several darker horizontal stripes on its sides. It grows to about 4 pounds in weight, and is most commonly taken incidentally to fishing for other species.

ROCKFISH FAMILY

Sebastes spp.

The largest fish family along the California coast is the rockfish. Any specimen caught that weighs more than 1 pound should be considered a rarity.

KELP ROCKFISH *Sebastes atrovirens* This member of the family is not much of a fighter. However, it makes an excellent fish for the table.

GRASS ROCKFISH *Sebastes rastrelliger* An able fighter, this fish will use every trick and take every opportunity to tangle the angler's line. Unfortunately, the flesh is considered nearly inedible.

CABEZON

Scorpaenichthys marmoratus

Surf anglers, particularly those fishing the rocky shores, take a good number of cabezon, one of about 60 members of the sulpin family found along the Pacific coast. It can occasionally grow to 25 pounds.

LEFT
Jack crevalle
≈

CREVALLE

Caranx hippos

Also known as the jack crevalle, horse crevalle and common jack, it is found in virtually all tropical and subtropical waters on Earth. Twenty-pounders are not at all unusual and they provide a battle beyond their size; 35- to 45-pound crevalle are taken each year in the waters around Florida.

The fish is bluish-black to greenish above and generally silver on its underside. It has a pug-type forehead and face, and very smooth sides.

SPANISH MACKEREL

Scomberomorus maculaturs

Similar to the wahoo, it sports a thin, elongated body. It differs from the closely related king mackerel and cero in that the side stripes are replaced with spots.

Ten-pounders are considered large, although fish reaching 20 pounds are taken regularly. This East Coast species is taken as far north as Cape Cod from June to September, and further south for longer periods of the year.

AMBERJACK

Seriola dumerili

This is another species that is found across the globe in tropical and warmer temperate waters. It is taken as far north as New York during the summer months.

Maximum weights of more than 150 pounds are common, although 30- to 60-pounders are much more common. A similar species, the Pacific amberjack (*Seriola colburni*) attains weights of just over 100 pounds maximum.

Although the amberjack is more commonly taken in deep waters, particularly over wrecks and at offshore oil rigs, it does move into the surf for feeding on occasion.

While the flesh is generally considered edible, it is also commonly infested with worms. Catch-and-release is generally advisable.

GREAT BARRACUDA

Sphyraena barracuda

This fish has a manmade reputation as dangerous because of its ample set of razor-sharp teeth and the fish can inflict nasty injuries; however, when handled properly the fish need not be feared.

Ranging as far north as North Carolina, the fish is quite common throughout the flats of the Florida Keys. It averages 5-10 pounds, although 20-pounders are not uncommon.

LITTLE TUNNY

Euthynnus alletteratus

This is readily identified by the cat-like markings along its back. While most of its tuna relatives are off-shore, deeper water species, the little tunny is commonly taken in the surf.

Although this Atlantic Coast species averages from 5 to 15 pounds and tops out at about 30 pounds, it is a terrific fighter on light tackle. Unfortunately, the little tunny's reputation on the table does not live up to its performance in the water.

Catch-and-release is probably advisable for those fish that have not worn themselves down too much in the battle.

CERO MACKEREL

Scomberomorus regalis

Also known as pintada and cero, these are found along the Atlantic coast from Cape Cod south. They are abundant in the waters of southern Florida. Fish of more than 35 pounds have been taken, although less than 10 pounds is much closer to the average.

The cero mackerel differs from both king and Spanish mackerel in its mixture of spots and stripes on its sides.

KING MACKEREL

Scomberomorus cavalla

Known as the kingfish, 5- to 15-pounder king mackerel were once taken in almost unbelievable numbers. Overfishing, however, has decimated its population and today's catches are maintained only through strict regulation.

ABOVE
Barracuda
≈

PINK SALMON

Oncorhynchus gorbuscha

Also known as the humpback salmon, this is one of the anadromous species of the Pacific Coast, migrating from the ocean into rivers at the age of two for spawning. Commonly taken at the mouths of rivers and upriver, the pink salmon is one of the smaller species, averaging about 5-6 pounds.

SPOT

Leiostomus xanthurus

This is a relatively tiny panfish that is as often used as bait as it ends up as table fare. It rarely reaches a pound, but is found in concentrated numbers along the Atlantic coast.

BONEFISH

Albula vulpes

This is the legendary species of the flats of the Florida Keys. It attracts anglers from around the world to do battle in the strange hunting-fishing method that has evolved, in which guides pole their boats along the flats searching for the quarry to which their clients will then cast. The fight is spectacular, complete with blistering runs.

The species average 3 to 8 pounds, with a maximum in the neighborhood of 20 pounds, but the specialized technique involved in catching it makes it a prized gamefish.

The species' first strike is often a spectacular leap at the bait or lure, followed by a powerful battle. It is an excellent fish for table fare. The king mackerel can be differentiated from similar species by the lack of spots along its sides.

SNOOK

Centropomus undecimalis

These are shallow-water fish, often taken well up into rivers, even in totally freshwater habitats. They are, however, extremely sensitive to drops in water temperature, and large winter kills occur regularly. They are easily identified by the black line along their scaly sides and their protruding lower jaw.

The species averages 5 to 20 pounds, but has been recorded at more than 50 pounds. Commonly found at manmade structures and around mangrove roots, snook are regularly taken on all sorts of artificial lures, but live bait remains the best bet.

ACROSS *THE*

CONTINENT

ALABAMA

Flounder, mullet, sand sea trout, croaker, spot and gafftopsail catfish, jack crevalle, red drum and several shark species are all common in Alabama's coastal waters. The spotted sea trout is extremely popular in the spring, and the average red drum caught during the fall is 18 pounds.

ALABAMA

The State also offers two public fishing piers: an 825-footer at Gulf State Park and the 665-footer at Dauphin Island. Migrating species, such as king mackerel and cobia, are regularly taken at Gulf State Park, and a spring cobia run produces fish in the 40- to 60-pound range. Both produce good night fishing for spotted sea trout and outstanding Spanish mackerel fishing, spring through fall.

For more information contact Alabama Bureau of Tourism and Travel, 532 S Perry St, Montgomery, AL 36104, 1–800–252–2262; Division of Marine Resources, Alabama Department of Conservation and Natural Resources, 64 N Union St, Montgomery, AL 36130; (205) 261–3346.

BELOW
A shark is brought onto the beach by a successful angler.

ALASKA

Salmon are king in these waters and much of the fishing in Alaska is done along its many rivers and by boat. However there is much action also available to the saltwater shoreline fisherman, as indicated by the following listing of prime fishing spots.

Significant fisheries of king salmon exist at Blind Slough, Herring Bay, and Wrangell Harbor and Narrows, with peak availability May through June. Sockeye salmon abound at Chilkoot Inlet, Lutak Inlet, Redoubt Bay, Sitkoh Bay, with the peak June through August; and Eshamy Bay and Lagoon, peak July through August. Coho salmon at Blind Slough, Herring Bay, and Wrangell Harbor and Narrows, peak in September; Auke Bay, Chilkat Inlet, Chilkoot Inlet, Gastineau Channel, Lutak Inlet, Shelter Island, Stephens Passage, Port Banks, Redoubt Bay, Sitka Sound and Whale Bay, peak August through September; Passage Canal and Valdez Arm, peak July through August; Kachemak Bay, Resurrection Bay and Cook Inlet, peak mid-July through early September. Pink salmon can be found at Clover Pass, Herring Bay, Mountain Point, and Wrangell Harbor and Narrows, peak July through early August; Auke Bay, Chilkat Inlet, Chilkoot Inlet, Gastineau Channel, Lutak Inlet, Shelter Island, Stephens Passage, Taiya Inlet and Sitka Sound, peak July; Valdez Arm, peak July through mid-August; Kachemak Bay, Resurrection Bay and Cook Inlet, peak late July through mid-August. Chum salmon are at Gastineau Channel and Stephens Passage, peak July.

Halibut are taken from shore at Sitka Sound year-round. Rockfish are caught at Wrangell Harbor and Narrows, Kelp Bay, Kha Sheets Bay, Peril Strait and Sitka Sound.

Dolly Varden are taken at Blind Slough, Clover Pass, Herring Bay, Mountain Point, Wrangell Harbor and Narrows, Auke Bay, Chilkat Inlet, Chilkoot Inlet, Gastineau Channel, Lutak Inlet, Shelter Island, Stephens Passage, Taiya Inlet, Tee Harbor, Redoubt Bay, Sitka Sound, Passage Canal, Pigot Bay, Cochrane Bay, Culross Passage, Long Bay, Main Bay, Eshamy Bay and Lagoon, Coghill Lagoon, Jackpot Bay, Knight Island, Patton Bay, Valdez Arm, Unakwik Inlet, Galena Bay, Simpson Bay and Hell's Hole. Flounder and sole are available at Passage Canal, Pigot Bay, Cochrane Bay, Culross Passage, Long Bay, Main Bay, Eshamy Bay and Lagoon, Coghill Lagoon, Jackpot Bay, Knight Island, Montague Island, Hinchinbrook Island, Valdez Arm and Unakwik Inlet.

For more information contact the Alaska Department of Fish and Game, PO Box 3–2000, Juneau, AS 99802–2000, (907) 465–4100.

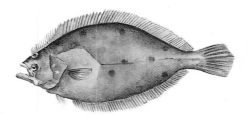

Summer Flounder

Red Drum

Blue Rockfish

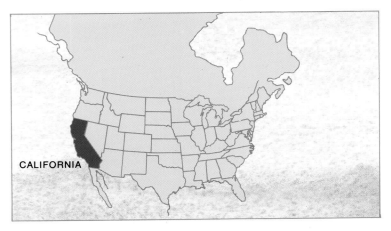

CALIFORNIA

DEL NORTE, HUMBOLDT AND MENDOCINO COUNTIES Spring and summer are the most popular times of the year for fishing the sandy beaches in these counties. The redtail surfperch that make up a vast majority of the catch are most available during March through May. Other species taken include the silver and walleye surf-perches and the starry flounder.

Some of the most productive beaches are Gold Bluff, Luffenholtz, Mad River, Centerville, Juan Creek, Howard Creek, Ten Mile River, MacKerricher State Park, Albion River and Alder Creek.

This region also offers about 120 miles of fine rocky shorelines, hosting species such as kelp greenling, jacksmelt, black rockfish, striped seaperch, rock greenling, redtail surfperch, blue rockfish, cabezon, lingcod and sculpin. Jetties, such as those at Buhne Point, Crescent City, Humboldt, Noyo Harbor and Fort Bragg, are productive for flounder, Pacific halibut, jacksmelt, walleye surfperch, shiner perch, sand sole, and several smaller species of sharks and rays.

Pier fishing in this region is relatively limited, although the piers that do exist seem to offer better than average catches of jacksmelt, true smelt, surf-perch, greenling, sea perch, cabezon and rockfish.

Public-owned piers are at Crescent City, but privately owned piers with public access can be found at Humboldt Bay, Noyo Harbor and Point Arena.

SONOMA AND MARIN COUNTIES The shoreline of these counties lends itself to a variety of shore-fishing methods because of the different physical features and species present, ranging from steelhead fishing at the mouths of rivers, through halibut fishing near outlets and shores of bays, to rockfish and surfperch fishing along the rocky shores.

Redtail surfperch are again a popular species, taken on sand crabs and cutfish. Russian River, Rodeo Lagoon Beach, Point Reyes Beach, Drakes Beach and Dillon Beach are popular areas, with February through June being the prime season.

This section of the coastline offers many rocky areas and a few artificial jetties, where kelp greenling, blue rockfish, striped sea perch, cabezon, rock greenling and black rockfish are taken on shrimp, cutfish, mussel, clam and abalone. A jetty is located at Bodega Bay.

Fishing piers in this region are generally small and privately owned. There is a public pier at San Pablo Bay.

Poke-poling is rumored to have developed along this section of the coast. The shallow rocky areas at Duxbury Reef, Tomales Point, Dillon Beach and Estero de San Antonio are favored at low tide. Monkeyface eels are the most abundant species available to these anglers.

SAN FRANCISCO, SAN MATEO AND SANTA CRUZ COUNTIES Striped bass are a popular quarry each year along the sandy beaches of these counties, and the Elkhorn Slough area of Monterey County, from May through October.

Redtail, calico and barred surfperch are readily available from Baker Beach south to Princeton. Jacksmelt, white croaker, starry flounder, sand sole, sharks and rays are also available.

The region offers extensive rocky coastal areas, but few that are not potentially dangerous and ravenous on gear. Jetties at Halfmoon Bay Harbor and Santa Cruz Small Craft Harbor are large but heavily fished. There is a rock fishery for striped bass between Baker Beach and Sutro's in San Francisco.

There are five public and three private fishing piers from San Francisco to Moss Landing. Striped bass are taken in appreciable numbers from the pier at Seacliff Beach State Park. Rock fill, under the San Francisco Municipal Pier, affords refuge for several species of rockfish, surfperch and greenling. White croaker, jacksmelt, barred surfperch, walleye surfperch, shiner perch and several species of flounder are taken over the sandy bottom at the Princeton piers. The Santa Cruz pier was built over sandy bottom but there has been a steady accumulation of debris, cement fill and the like, creating habitat for several rock-dwelling species including cabezon, lingcod and greenling. Capitola Pier is over a sandy bottom and walleye surfperch, white croaker and jacksmelt are the primary species.

The Cement Ship is on sand but the central wells of the ship afford habitat for a variety of species such as rainbow sea perch, pile perch and striped sea perch. Moss Landing Pier is in deep water over a sandy bottom and attracts several deeper-water species such as small sablefish and bocaccio.

MONTEREY AND SAN LUIS OBISPO COUNTIES In these counties striped bass fishing is erratic between Moss Landing and Monterey. Good runs occur but usually are short-lived. The beach off Seaside is the southernmost area where large shore concentrations occur along the Pacific coast.

Barred surfperch are the most important sport fish in the surf of sandy beaches in this region, with the best catches coming in May through August. Walleye, silver and calico surfperch are also taken.

Rocky area fishing is most popular on the Mont-

erey Peninsula between Cannery Row and Yankee Point, where much of the shoreline is available to the public. South of Yankee Point only a few rocky areas are open to the public. The area from Piedras Blancas Point south is open to the public except for military and private holdings.

There are 10 fishing piers in the region: Moss Landing, two at Monterey, San Simeon, Cayucos, two at Morro Bay, two at Avila, and Pismo Beach. Fishing at Monterey and Cayucos piers is erratic. The average catch is relatively low, but heavy concentrations of bocaccio, jacksmelt and surfperch may move through the area during the summer.

LOS ANGELES COUNTY This is the most populous and heavily developed region of the Pacific coastline, but it does offer some good surf fishing spots. From the San Gabriel River to the Los Angeles River, the coastline is marked by wide, sandy beaches with little surf action, due to the presence of the Long Beach–San Pedro breakwaters. However, surfperch and corbina are commonly caught from these beaches. The steep, rugged bluffs and rock-strewn shoreline of the Palos Verdes Peninsula are the top surf waters of this region, producing excellent catches of corbina and barred surfperch. Opaleye, barred sand bass and kelp bass are commonly taken from the many jetties throughout this region.

ORANGE AND SAN DIEGO COUNTIES The white croaker is among the most common species caught from shore in these counties. Barred surfperch, queenfish, fornia corbina, opaleye, black surfperch, spotfin croaker and walleye surfperch are also taken regularly.

Piers and jetties throughout this region produce queenfish, white croaker, walleye surfperch, shiner surfperch, jacksmelt, topsmelt, halibut, Pacific mackerel, kelp bass, bonito and barracuda.

For more information contact California Department of Fish and Game, 1416 Ninth St, Sacramento, CA 95814, (916) 445–7613.

ABOVE

A surf fisherman waits for the strike along Limantour Beach, part of the Point Reyes National Seashore.

ACROSS THE CONTINENT

71

Lingcod

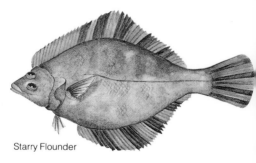

Starry Flounder

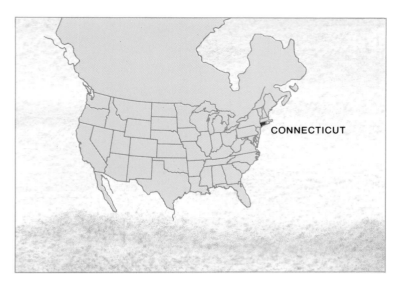

CONNECTICUT

Long Island Sound prevents the coastline of Connecticut from getting surf conditions in all but the windiest of conditions. And, access to the shoreline is quite restricted. Nevertheless, stripers, blues, flounder, tautog and mackerel can all be taken from the shore areas.

For more information contact Fisheries Bureau, Connecticut Department of Environmental Protection, State Office Building, 165 Capitol Ave, Hartford, CN 06106, (203) 566–2287

DELAWARE

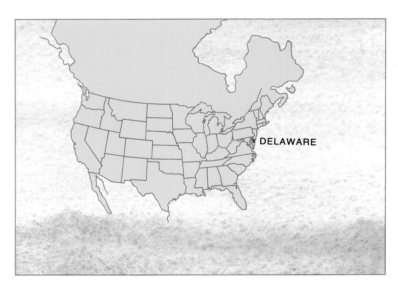

Only a small portion of Delaware's coastline is exposed to the Atlantic Ocean proper; most is instead bordered along the Delaware Bay. Both areas are productive for surf and shore fishermen.

The Atlantic mackerel arrive in April to begin the season, which runs through November, when the final schools of bluefish and weakfish swim south. Weakfish are especially abundant from mid-May through summer. The tautog is popular in the waters off Lewes as fall arrives.

Rehoboth Beach to the Indian River offers good access to the beach, and the jetties at Indian River can be productive.

For more information contact Division of Fish and Wildlife, Delaware Department of Natural Resources and Environmental Control, 89 Kings Highway, PO Box 1401, Dover, DE 19903, (302) 736–5295; Delaware Sea Grant College Program, University of Delaware, Newark, DE 19716, (302) 451–2841.

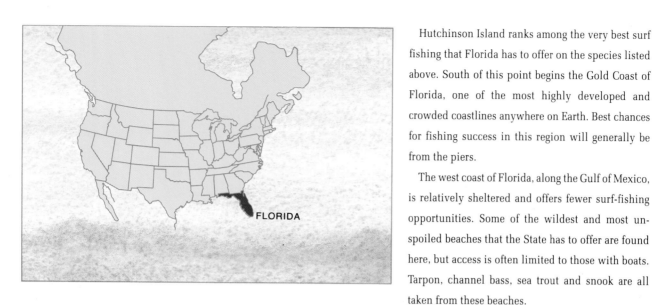

FLORIDA

≈

Surrounded on three sides by ocean, Florida offers some of the most extensive beaches for surf fishing in North America. Development, however, is quickly taking a toll on public access to these areas.

Tarpon, black drum, channel bass, sea trout, sheepshead, whiting and cobia are common along the beaches and jetties as far south as New Smyrna Beach. They are joined by bluefish, snook, pompano and jacks further south.

Hutchinson Island ranks among the very best surf fishing that Florida has to offer on the species listed above. South of this point begins the Gold Coast of Florida, one of the most highly developed and crowded coastlines anywhere on Earth. Best chances for fishing success in this region will generally be from the piers.

The west coast of Florida, along the Gulf of Mexico, is relatively sheltered and offers fewer surf-fishing opportunities. Some of the wildest and most un-spoiled beaches that the State has to offer are found here, but access is often limited to those with boats. Tarpon, channel bass, sea trout and snook are all taken from these beaches.

Probably the best surf fishing that Florida's share of the Gulf of Mexico coastline has is found in the Panama City area. Cobia, sea trout, channel bass, jacks, pompano, whiting and bluefish are taken here, almost year-round.

For more information contact Division of Marine Resources and Division of Beaches and Shores, Florida Department of Natural Resources, Marjory Stoneman Douglas Building, Tallahassee, FL 32303, (904) 488–6058; Sea Grant Extension Program, 117 Newins/Ziegler Hall, University of Florida, Gainesville, FL 32611, (904) 392–1837.

BELOW
Snook

GEORGIA

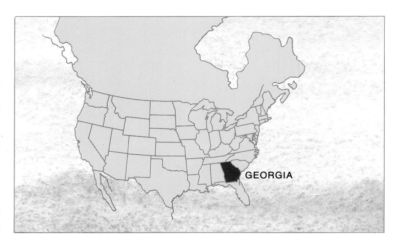

GEORGIA

Many miles of streams meander through 4½ million acres of salt marshes along the Georgia coastline before draining into the Atlantic Ocean. This environment is vital to many species of marine life and it is often referred to as a nursery ground.

This intricate network of streams poses a formidable obstacle to anglers, but the surf fishing waiting on the other side is definitely worth the effort. Prime surf-fishing locations include the outlets of Altahama and St Simon's Sounds and Hampton River.

The Atlantic croaker is one of the most abundant fish species along the Georgia coastline. It begins to become available to fishermen in March and is quite abundant by late March and April. In the summer this species moves into the shallows surrounding the sounds and adjacent waters, and in October it begins to move into deeper waters for the winter.

The black drum is most abundant in Georgia waters in April and May, when the species congregates for spawning. This fish is fairly common during the summer months in the sounds and nearby streams as well as along the outer beaches of the barrier islands.

The sheepshead gathers in loose schools each spring in shallow waters near sandy shores, but after spawning returns to the preferred habitat along breakwaters, jetties, dock pilings and oyster reefs. It is generally a loner species during the non-spawning period.

Kingfish, also known as whiting, are common along the State's beaches during summer and fall. They often swim in the surf zone so close to shore that they are temporarily stranded in the wake of receding waves.

Red drum are most abundant in or just beyond the surf zone along the outer beaches of the barrier

islands lining Georgia's coast. They are taken more commonly during the warmer months.

The spotted sea trout is one of the most sought-after sportfish in all the southeastern United States, including Georgia. It is an estuarine species, spending all of its life in bays, sounds, rivers and creeks bordered by marsh grass.

Both the summer flounder and the southern flounder are abundant in Georgia waters. They are taken on a large variety of bait and tackle.

The distribution of the striped bass is patchy at best in these southern waters, apparently confined to the major rivers and the estuaries immediately adjacent to them. The Georgia Game and Fish Commission has maintained an active hatching and stocking program since 1969, concentrating on the Savannah, Altamaha and Ogeechee Rivers to augment existing populations.

Several species of shark are also found in Georgia's coastal waters. They are most commonly taken at the outlets of the sounds and rivers.

More information is available from Coastal Resources Division, Georgia Department of Natural Resources, Floyd Towers East, 205 Butler St, Atlanta, GA 30334, (912) 264–7221; University of Georgia, Marine Sciences Program, Ecology Building, Athens, GA 30602, (404) 542–7671.

LOUISIANA

≈

Due to the effects of the Mississippi and several other rivers as they empty into the Gulf of Mexico through this State, Louisiana's coastline is pretty much unlike any other coastal environment to be found in North America. Rivers, marshes, bayous and protected bays are the norm in Louisiana, rather than beach.

Many of the islands in the State's coastal waters provide fine surf fishing, but access is generally limited to boat or plane except in a few locations. Noteworthy among these islands are the Chandeleur chain to the east and the Casse-tetes to the south, where channel bass, flounder, sea trout and pompano are abundant. The waters around Marsh Island have shown a definite attraction for some shallow-water shark species.

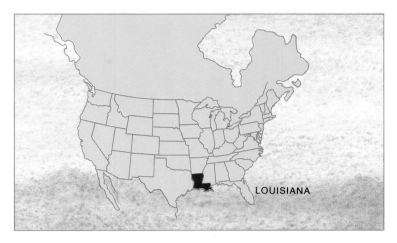

For more information contact Louisiana Department of Wildlife and Fisheries, PO Box 15570, Baton Rouge, LA 70895, (504) 765–2800; Sea Grant College Program, Center of Wetland Resources, Louisiana State University, Baton Rouge, LA 70803, (504) 388–6710.

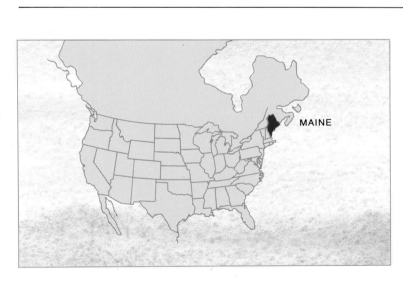

MAINE

≈

Like much of Canada, the coastline of Maine has never been as fully developed from a surf-fishing standpoint as many other areas of the North American coast. That does not mean that the fish are not there to be had. Striped bass can be taken much of the year; mackerel are commonly caught throughout the summer; and good numbers of flounder, tautog and pollock are available.

Popular spots include Kennebunk Beach, Popham Beach, Higgins Beach, York Beach, Parsons Beach, Ocean Park, Old Orchard Road, Camp Ellis and the mouths of rivers such as the Kennebec, Morse, Belfast, York, Mousam, Ogunquit, Kennebunk, Saco, Darmariscotta and Scarboro.

For more information contact Maine Department of Marine Resources, State House, Station No 21, Augusta, ME 04333, (207) 289–2291; Maine Atlantic Sea Run Salmon Commission, PO Box 1298, Hedin Hall, Bangor, ME 04401, (207) 941–4449; Sea Grant Program, Microbiology Department, University of Maine, Orono, ME 04469, (207) 581–2802.

MARYLAND

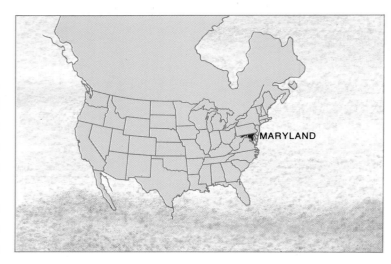

Striped bass, channel bass, bluefish, weakfish, summer flounder, tautog, kingfish, croaker, and several species of shark are commonly caught in the limited surf waters of Maryland. Some of these same species are taken in respectable numbers in the Chesapeake Bay as well.

Assateague and Paramore Islands are both popular spots favored by surf fishermen, as are the waters around Cape Charles. In addition, the Chesapeake Bay Bridge–Tunnel offers shore anglers some access to much deeper waters, which are totally inaccessible elsewhere.

For more information contact Maryland Department of Natural Resources, Tawes State Office Building, Annapolis, MD 21401, (301) 974–3041; Sea Grant College, University of Maryland, College Park, MD 20742, (301) 454–5690; Chesapeake Bay Foundation Inc, 162 Prince George St, Annapolis, MD 21401, (301) 268–8816.

MASSACHUSETTS

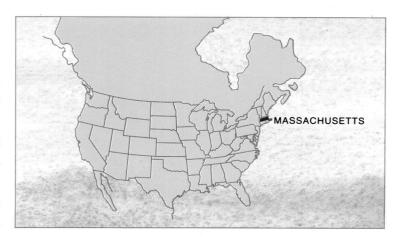

Striped bass is the most popular surf species along the Massachusetts coast, and for good reason. The fish can be had in relatively good numbers in this region. Cape Cod offers many famous surf fishing spots, such as Peaked Hill, Race Point, Race Point Lighthouse, Nauset Light, Chatham Island, North Truro, Wellfleet, Monomoy Island and Orleans. Bluefish are also available in these locations, and pollock are taken during the spring at Race Point. In addition, some of the famous offshore islands, like Nantucket and Martha's Vineyard are famous for the striper and bluefish fishing in their waters, particularly in June through October.

For more information contact Division of Marine Fisheries, Massachusetts Department of Fisheries, Wildlife and Environmental Law Enforcement, 100 Cambridge St, Boston, MA 02202, (617) 727–3193; Sea Grant College Program, Massachusetts Institute of Technology, Building E38, Room 302, Cambridge, MA 02139, (617) 253–7042.

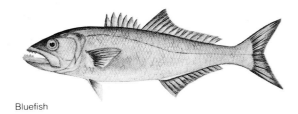

Bluefish

MISSISSIPPI

Mississippi offers few fishable beaches, with the State's best surf fishing coming on the offshore islands that are mostly only accessible by boat or plane. Notable among these are Horn, Ship, Petit Bois and Cat Islands.

Most species of the Gulf of Mexico are regularly taken in the surf on these islands.

For more information contact Mississippi Department of Wildlife Conservation, Southport Mall, PO Box 451, Jackson, MS 39205, (601) 362–9212; Gulf Coast Research Laboratory, Ocean Springs, MS 39564, (601) 875–2244; Mississippi-Alabama Sea Grant Consortium, Caylor Building, Gulf Coast Research Laboratory, Ocean Springs, MS 39564, (601) 875–9341.

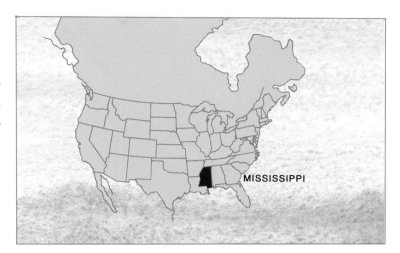

NEW HAMPSHIRE

The New Hampshire coast is extremely limited, but it does offer fishing for striped bass, mackerel, pollock, salmon, and a few other species. Top spots are the mouths of the Piscataqua and Hampton Rivers, Rye Beach, Seabrook Beach, Rye Harbor State Park and Hampton Beach.

For more information contact Inland and Marine Fisheries Division, New Hampshire Fish and Game Department, 34 Bridge St, Concord, NH 03301, (603) 868–1096; University of New Hampshire/University of Maine Joint Sea Grant College Program, University of New Hampshire, Durham, NH 03824, (603) 862–2996.

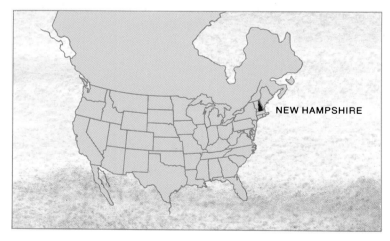

Pollock

NEW JERSEY

≈

"The Jersey Shore," as the coastline of this small State is known to many in the northeastern United States, is a highly commercialized affair, catering to every tourist interest, including surf fishing.

Substantial surf fishing areas in New Jersey are found at Asbury Park, Atlantic City, Barnegut Light, Beach Haven, Belmar, Brant Beach, Brigantine, Cape May, Island Beach State Park, Lavellette, Long Branch, Manasquan, Ocean City, Sea Bright, Sea Isle City, Seaside Heights, Ship Bottom, Stone Harbour, Surf City and Wildwood.

The most popular jetties are located at Asbury Park, Atlantic City, Barnegut Light, Belmar, Brigantine, Cape May, Island Beach State Park, Long Branch, Manasquan, Sea Bright and Surf City. Piers are available at Asbury Park, Atlantic City, Atlantic Highlands, Barnegut Light, Belmar, Brigantine, Keyport, Long Branch, Ocean City, Seaside Heights, Ventnor and Wildwood. Most are commercially operated and charge a fee.

Fish species generally available to surf and bay fishermen, and the periods in which they are most commonly taken are: blowfish, May through August; bluefish, May through November; croaker, July through September; drum, May and June; fluke, June through October; kingfish, July through September; mackerel, April and May; porgy, June through October; seabass, May through September; shark, June through October; spot, June through September; striped bass, March through December; tautog, April through November; weakfish, May through November; whiting, January through May, and November through December; white perch, year-round; winter flounder, January through May, and November through December.

NEW JERSEY

For more information contact Publications, Nacote Creek Marine Laboratory, Star Route, Absecon, NJ 08201; Division of Fish, Game and Wildlife, New Jersey Department of Environmental Protection, 401 E State St, CN 400, Trenton, NJ 08625, (609) 292–2965; New Jersey Marine Science Consortium, Fort Hancock, NJ 07732, (201) 872–1300.

BELOW
A flock of seabirds pinpoints a school of bluefish for this angler at Seaside Park, New Jersey.

≈

NEW YORK

NEW YORK

The waters of the 2,200 miles of shoreline around Long Island are among the most heavily fished in the world, but they continue to produce excellent catches on many different species. Dozens of line-class world record fish have been taken here. Many municipal, State and Federal beaches, parks and recreational areas provide ready access to the surf and to protected bay areas. Fluke, flounder, black-fish, bluefish, weakfish and porgie are abundant.

The Hudson River, which empties into the Atlantic Ocean at the southern tip of Long Island, is "one of the most prolific spawning and nursery areas" for striped bass along the Atlantic Coast, according to *The Conservationist*, the magazine of the State Department of Environmental Conservation.

The surf calendar: January and February, primarily whiting and herring from piers; March through May, cod, pollock and large winter flounder (April into May, mackerel and fluke join the action); mid- to late May, porgies and striped bass begin; June, fluke, weakfish, blowfish, kingfish, winter flounder and blackfish; July and August, similar to June with more small blues; September, small bluefish are at their peak and stripers are becoming more abundant; October, winter flounder and stripers; November,

winter flounder at its best through the middle of the month and bluefish blitzes will continue through until Thanksgiving Day; December, almost exclusively flounder.

Additional, more specific, information is available from the New York State Department of Environmental Conservation, Division of Marine Resources, SUNY, Building 40, Stony Brook, NY 11794, (516) 751–7900; Long Island Tourism and Convention Commission, 213 Carleton Ave, Center Islip, NY 11772; (516) 234–4959; Marine Sciences Research Center, SUNY, Stony Brook, NY 11794, (516) 632–8700; New York Sea Grant Institute, SUNY and Cornell University, Stony Brook, NY 11794, (516) 632–6905.

NORTH CAROLINA

≈

The world-famous Outer Banks, which are a broken chain of sandy, barrier islands that stretch from the Virginia State line to Morehead City, offer more than 100 miles of accessible beach as well as eight fishing piers; some of these piers extend more than 1,000 feet into the water. The seasonal peaks for surf fishing are mid-March through May, and September through November.

The spring season offers an abundance of channel bass, some tipping the scales at more than 60 pounds, as well as flounder, whiting, spot, bluefish, sea trout and croakers. The "big blues" are popular at this time of the year, growing more evident each spring, although their size is generally greater in fall.

Smaller bluefish, Spanish mackerel and flounder keep the action going through the summer months, along with some croaker, spot and gray trout. However, fishing at this time cannot be rated anything better than fair.

The action begins to pick up in August when pompano and Spanish mackerel move onto the scene. A few tarpon have been taken at this time of the year, on live baits floated for king mackerel.

Pompano and tarpon are at their best in September. At this time the channel bass and big blues return, and flounder, spot, croaker, gray trout and false albacore become abundant. Bluefish of more than 15 pounds are regular occurences. Striped bass begin to appear, with irregularity, with the end of the month, particularly around Hatteras Island, where bluefish are so plentiful as to be considered a nuisance by some.

Cutbait, bloodworms, squid and shrimp are the popular naturals, while metal casting lures are effective on mackerel and big blues.

Guide service is available at several points, includ-

NORTH CAROLINA

ing Nags Head, Buxton, Ocracoke and Core Banks, at rates ranging to $175 per day for a party of three or four anglers. The guides generally provide vehicle, fuel, tackle and bait.

Top spots are near the inlets, notably Drum Inlet, Ocracoke Inlet, Hatteras Inlet, Oregon Inlet and Beaufort Inlet.

For more information contact North Carolina Wildlife Resources Commission, Archdale Building, 512 N Salisbury St, Raleigh, NC 27611, (919) 733–3391; University of North Carolina Sea Grant College Program, Box 8605, North Carolina State University, Raleigh, NC 27695–8605, (919) 737–2454; Outer Banks Chamber of Commerce, PO Box 90, Kitty Hawk, NC 27949, (919) 995–4213; Dare County Tourist Bureau, PO Box 399, Manteo, NC 27954, (919) 473–2138; North Carolina Travel and Tourism Division, 430 N Salisbury St, Raleigh, NC 27611, 1–800–438–4404.

BELOW

Two anglers cast baitfish into the waters at Ocracoke Island, North Carolina, in pursuit of channel bass.

≈

OREGON

Striped bass fishing in the surf has been coming on strong in the coastal waters of this northwestern State in recent years, where most stripers were previously taken from boat.

Like a few other northerly states, Oregon's waters – particularly at the mouths of rivers – provide the added excitement and incentive of fishing for spawn-run salmon and steelhead. Rocky points, jetties and the beaches at these points are all excellent choices for anglers.

Other species taken along this mostly rocky coastline include surfperches of several species, rockfish, cabazone and greenling. Access to the beaches and rocky shores is generally easy, as the State has made many parks available.

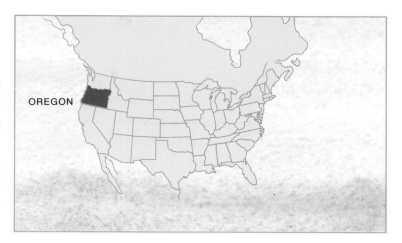

For more information contact Oregon Department of Fish and Wildlife, 107 20th St, La Grande, OR 97850, (503) 229–5551; Sea Grant College program, Administrative Services Building, A320, Oregon State University, Corvallis, OR 97331, (503) 754–2714.

RHODE ISLAND

The size of tiny Rhode Island is in no way reflected in its surf fishery, which is among the best along the entire Atlantic coast. Striped bass, summer flounder, mackerel, tautog, pollock and weakfish are all taken from its variety of sandy beaches, rocky shores and many jetties.

The rocky shores are found more commonly along the northern portion of the State's coastline in places such as Flat Rock, Hazard Avenue, Stewart's Stinky Beach, Point Judith, Narrow River, Ocean Drive, Fort Varnum, Sheep-pen, Dunes Club Beach, Monahan's Cove and the Clumps.

Sandy beaches are found more southerly, including Green Hill, Breakway, Charlestown Beach, Quonochontaug, Misquamicut, Mantunuck Beach,

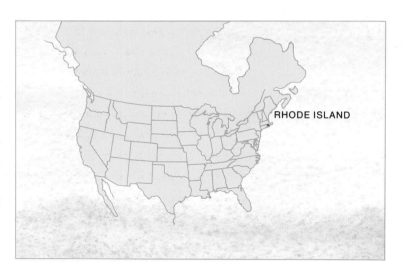

East Beech, Qyonochontaug and Weekapaug.

For more information contact Division of Coastal Resources, Rhode Island Department of Environmental Management, 22 Hayes St, Providence, RI 02908, (401) 277–3429.

SOUTH CAROLINA

≈

Spotted sea trout come off a long winter of relative
inactivity quite hungry in late March and early April,
beginning in the upper reaches of the estuaries.
Shrimp and baitfish float-fished or bottom-fished, as
well as artificial lures, will prove effective.

Trophy red drum of up to and more than 30 pounds
begin to reappear at this same time in the surf, offering the best fishing with the incoming tide in deep
holes. Cutbait fished on the bottom is the preferred
method.

Migrating bluefish come onto the scene in April
and May, frequenting areas of strong current. A hot-
spot is the south jetty at the mouth of Charleston
Harbor during low tide. A favored artificial lure in
the topwater popper plug, Striper Swiper.

SOUTH CAROLINA

For more information: South Carolina Wildlife &
Marine Resources Department, Marine Resources
Division, PO Box 12559, Charleston, SC 29412, (803)
795–6350; Sea Grant Consortium, 287 Meeting St,
Charleston, SC 29401, (803) 727–2078.

RIGHT
Northern sea trout

≈

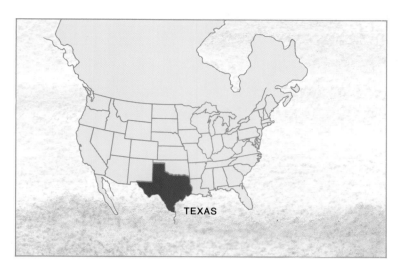

TEXAS

Many of the beaches of the Texas coastline are relatively undeveloped and offer a relaxing, wild experience while requiring some additional effort to access them. Much of this coastline comprises barrier islands.

Padre Island is among the top surf fishing spots in Texas. Although it is a heavily fished area, the beach remains in a wild state under protection as a National Seashore. Sharks, jacks, channel bass, sea trout, whiting, black drum, gafftopsail catfish, croaker and bluefish are relatively abundant here.

Sea trout are at their peak June through mid-July, and early October through early November; redfish, mid-February through early April, and October through mid-December; flounder, mid-September through mid-December; black drum, February through mid-April, and November through early December; croaker, mid-May through mid-July, and October; pompano, April through May, and late August through early November; sheepshead, early November through late February; Spanish mackerel, April through May, and August through September; tarpon, mid-May through early July, and late September through early November.

Jewfish and several species of shark are taken off the many jetties along the Texas coast. The mouth of Rio Grande River, which forms the Texan-Mexico border, offers sea trout, tarpon, redfish and snook.

For more information contact Texas Parks and Wildlife Department, 4200 Smith School Road, Austin, TX 78744, (512) 389–4800; Sea Grant College Program, Texas A&M University, College Station, TX 77843, (409) 845–3854.

BELOW

The catch is nice, but there are many other aspects to the sport, including the comradery of an able partner.

VIRGINIA

The top surf fishing in Virginia's waters is found on the barrier islands, which have access only via boat. Myrtle, Ship Shoal, Smith, Metomkin, Parramore, Hog, Cobb and Fisherman's Islands provide the best fishing for channel bass in the spring and fall. Other species commonly taken in the surf here include stripers, black drum, sea trout, kingfish, bluefish, croaker, flounder and weakfish.

Resort areas like Virginia Beach also offer some beach-fishing areas and piers.

For more information contact Virginia Marine Resources Commission, PO Box 756, 2401 West Ave, Newport News, VA 23608, (804) 257–0056; Virginia Graduate Marine Science Consortium, 170 Rugby Road, Madison House, University of Virginia, Charlottesville, VA 22903, (804) 924–5965.

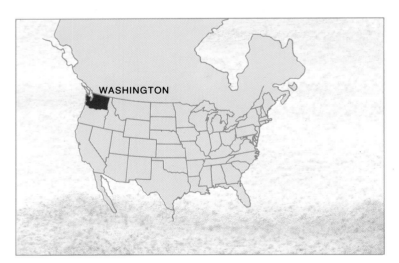

WASHINGTON

The coastline of Washington State is much like that of its southern neighbor, Oregon, but with many more bays and inlets that all generally offer prime opportunities for the surf and shore angler. Many jetties have been constructed in these areas.

The jetty at the mouth of the Columbia River deserves particular mention for its excellent salmon, surfperch and rockfish fishery. The same species, plus flounder and lingcod, are also abundant throughout the Juan de Fuca Strait.

For more information contact Washington Department of Fisheries, 115 General Administration Building, Olympia, WA 98504, (206) 753–6600; Sea Grant Program, University of Washington, 3716 Brooklyn Ave, NE, Seattle, WA 98105, (206) 543–6600.

CANADA — ATLANTIC COAST

Surf fishing is a growing sport, still closer to infancy than adulthood, throughout the coastal waters of Canada. Monster Atlantic salmon, taken in the many rivers of the region, are the focal point of sport angling. Saltwater fishing is largely dominated by charter boat activity.

Bluefish, rainbow smelt, Atlantic mackerel, striped bass, pollock, haddock, cod and American eel are among the common surf-area species taken along Canada's Atlantic coast.

For more information contact Department of Fisheries and Oceans, Scotia-Fundy Region, PO Box 550, Halifax, NS B3J 2S7; Nova Scotia Department of Fisheries, Purdy's Wharf, Third Floor, 1959 Upper Water Street, PO Box 2223, Halifax, NS B3J 3C4; Nova Scotia Department of Tourism, 5151 Terminal Road, PO Box 456, Halifax, NS B3J 2R5; Department of Natural Resources and Energy, PO Box 6000, Fredericton, NB, Canada, E3B 5H1, (506) 453–2440; Wildlife Division, Department of Culture, Recreation and Youth, Building 810, Pleasantville, PO Box 4750, St John's, NF A1C 5T7, (709) 576–2817.

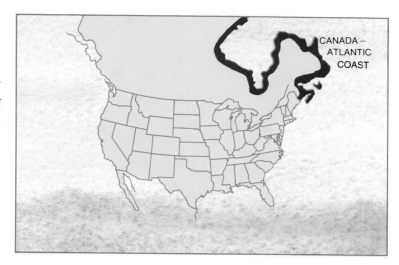

CANADA – ATLANTIC COAST

BELOW

King mackerel

≈

LEFT
An angler cleans a
beautiful pink salmon fillet
along the Johnstone Strait
in British Columbia,
Canada.

CANADA — PACIFIC COAST

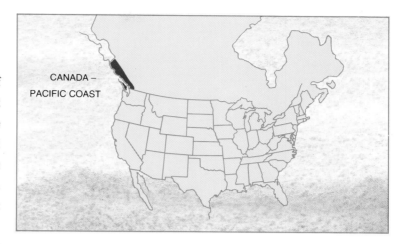

CANADA —
PACIFIC COAST

Any mention of the Canadian west coast must of course include Vancouver Island and its excellent Coho salmon fishery which is available to shore fishermen. The extraordinary number of inlets and river mouths to be found along this entire coastline act as an enormous magnet for many species of fish, including salmon, surfperch, rockfish, flounder and lingcod.

The fishing experience here is among the wildest that any coastline can offer; however, for the most part, access is severely limited. Boat and plane are the principal forms of transportation throughout this isolated region.

For more information on fishing the Pacific coast of Canada, anglers can contact Fisheries and Oceans, Ottawa, Ontario, Canada K1A 0E6, (613) 993–0600; Ministry of Environment and Parks, Parliament Buildings, Victoria, BC, Canada V8V 1X5, (604) 387–9507.

BELOW
A lone angler works a rocky point in Johnstone Strait, British Columbia, Canada.

THE FUTURE OF
SURF FISHING

Times are changing down by the old seaside. What we once thought of as a limitless larder of an almost endless array of an equally endless number of species now has been shown most definitely to have its natural limits.

Over-harvest and pollution have taken a heavier toll than anyone imagined they ever could, even a generation ago. Not only have we taken more from the oceans than we should have, we have used the waters as an enormous sewage tank, somehow believing that the oceans would make our most deadly concoctions magically disappear.

Both practices have impacted our fishery resources to a great, negative extent. Massive declines have already been noted in some of the most popular gamefish species. Some of the varieties most affected include striped bass, snook, red drum and king mackerel.

But we may not yet be past the point of no return, at least for many species. Catch-and-release is a relatively new concept for saltwater fishing in general and surf fishing in particular. While this renewable attitude has been growing for several generations of freshwater fishermen, the oceans have generally been viewed as inexhaustible, bottomless larders. In recent years however we've seen that this way of thinking is as outdated as some of the monster catches of yesteryear. This becomes evident as both size and numbers have been dropping for many of our most popular sport fish.

BELOW
Biologists are at work on many species today, such as these sharks, in an effort to learn more about the fish and the numbers that can be taken without damaging their populations.

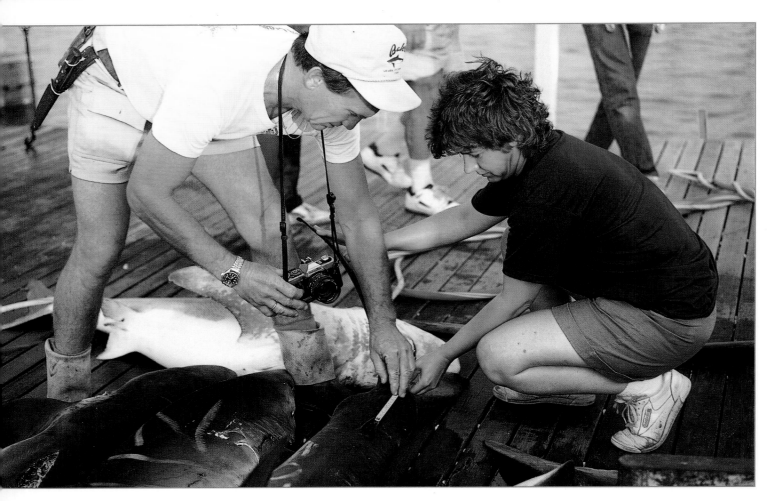

LEFT
Quick release of this fish
will help to continue the
sport for future years and
future generations.

Regulations have begun to surface to place size and number limits on the fish, and many anglers have turned to the catch-and-release philosophy. There are several basic concepts that must be kept in mind by the angler wanting to do his part in this way. The following pointers are offered by the Alaska Department of Fish and Game:

TACKLE: Strong line should be used to bring the fish in as quickly as possible. Fish taken on artificial lures and flies have a much better chance of survival than those taken on baits. Overly large hooks can damage mouthparts and eyes. By the same token, overly small hooks can be taken too deeply by the fish. The barbs of all hooks should be pinched down with pliers.

LANDING: The fish should be landed as quickly and carefully as possible. If at all possible, the fish should not be removed from the water. The fish should not be allowed to flop about in shallow water, over rocks or on dry land.

RIGHT

Needle-nose pliers can
help in the removal of
hooks while allowing safe
distance from the sharp
teeth with which many
saltwater species are
armed.

HANDLING THE CATCH: Keep the fish in the water.
Cradle it gently with both hands, one under the belly
and the other near its tail. Do not put your fingers in
its gills.

Use wet, cloth gloves or wet your hands to handle
the fish. Do not squeeze the fish. To take photos,
support the fish in the water. Cradle it carefully
while someone snaps the shot of the two of you
together.

REMOVING THE HOOK: Keeping the fish underwater,
remove the hook as quickly and gently as possible.
Back the hook out of its insertion point with long-
nosed pliers or hemostat. If the fish is hooked
deeply, cut the line as near as possible to the hook
and leave the hook in the fish. Steel hooks will rust
out of the fish much faster than hooks coated with
anti-rust material. Cut your line rather than injure
an active fish.

REVIVING THE FISH: Most fish taken in the surf will have put up a good battle and spent a lot of energy. They will require some resuscitation before release. Point the fish into a slow current or gently move it back and forth until its gills are working properly and the fish maintains its balance on its own. When the fish recovers and attempts to swim out of your hands, let it go. Large fish often taken longer to revive.

Another relatively new aspect to saltwater angling has been the growing concern over contamination in the fish that we are catching and eating.

State health departments have begun issuing health advisories about fish taken in specific waters, and in general in the waters of their States. Fish agencies now offer guidelines on filleting techniques that might lessen the amount of toxics in the fish that an angler consumes.

This may seem to be a problem more for the heavily industrialized areas of our coastlines. But, the oceans' waters know no real boundaries and, as a result, the assumption that any area is completely safe is a dangerous leap of faith in all situations. Check with the health department and fish agency with jurisdiction over the area you plan to fish.

ABOVE
Although catch-and-release needs to be more a part of the surf fisherman's vocabulary, it is still perfectly acceptable to take a meal of fish every now and again.

LEFT
Cleaning the catch may not be the most enjoyable part of the sport, but for those that choose to keep their fish it just can't be avoided.

INDEX